Winning with AB32

Winning with AB32

How to be a Winner in California's Cap & Trade System

By

Paul Hullar

Illustrations by Stephanie Carol

Cover Design and Graphics by Stephanie Carol

Diagrams by Stephanie Carol

ISBN: 978-0-615-88448-6

Table of Contents

About the Author

Paul Hullar graduated from Purdue University with a Bachelor's Degree in Chemical Engineering in 1985. He received a second degree in the Industry Cooperative Education Program in Engineering for the work that he completed at the Eastman Kodak Company. After graduation, Paul began his 25-year career at Procter & Gamble, where he led operations in their manufacturing plants in Green Bay, WI; Cape Girardeau, MO; Mehoopany, PA; and Oxnard, CA.

In 2006 while he was in Oxnard, Paul was asked to develop and lead a new Energy Conservation Program for Procter & Gamble's Family Care plants. These 5 Family Care paper plants, as designed, were very large and used a great deal of energy. In fact, they used half of Procter & Gamble' purchased energy worldwide. The remaining 129 plants collectively used the other half.

With a blank canvas to work from, Paul was able to study what the world-class companies around the world were doing and literally reapply the very best aspects of each program. He was also able to design the work processes within the new Energy Conservation Program to integrate with existing High Performance Work Systems, Safety Systems, Financial Systems, Maintenance Systems, and Training Systems.

This integrated approach allowed the Energy Conservation efforts to become a part of nearly every employee's work. This allowed it to become part of the Family Care culture.

In 2008 Paul helped couple the Energy Conservation Program with the company's Alternative Energy Program and the synergy of combining the two efforts delivered immediate improvements. In 2009 Paul's responsibilities increased further, providing direction for all 134 Procter & Gamble facilities world-wide. The best learnings from each plant and geography were documented, verified, and then rapidly reapplied to all other plants.

Although a web-based system was developed to house all of the tools, documents, and results, Paul always believed in a very hands-on approach to executing the work, personally conducting 12-15 audits annually in the plants.

The results were very satisfying, delivering $230 million in bottom line savings in 3 years. The Family Care plants enjoyed a 26% decrease in energy usage and a 35% reduction in CO_2 emissions.

In 2010 Paul saw the opportunity to use these strategies and tools that he had developed to help a larger number of plants achieve the same results. In December of that year, Paul founded Brightwave Energy, a consulting firm focused on helping manufacturing companies reduce their energy costs. The goal was simple: Reduce the manufacturing energy costs while being transparent to the customer or the consumer.

Brightwave Energy opened their doors for business in January 2011. In their first year, the Pacific Coast Business Times recognized Brightwave Energy in "Who's Who in Clean Tech and Sustainability". In 2012 and 2013 they were further recognized as "Leaders in Clean Technology".

Paul has led energy projects in the United States, Canada, Mexico, England, Germany, Italy, France, and Poland. He has been recognized three times in the Pacific Coast Business Times, contributed Op-Eds, and has spoken at events for the Ventura Chamber of Commerce, the Ventura County Economic Development Association, and the Fox Valley Center of Excellence.

Paul is passionate about Energy Conservation and helping businesses save money. He is also about passionate

Alternative and Advanced Fuels, and helping businesses reduce their CO_2 footprint if it can be monetized. Furthermore, Paul's strong sense of patriotism drives him to support efforts for national energy independence, and the reduced need to rely on foreign fuels.

"Winning with AB32" Op-Ed

"Winning with AB32"

California's "Global Warming Solutions Act" of 2006, also known as AB32, is generally regarded as unfriendly to businesses. However, as with many regulations, there will be Winners and Losers. There are more than 360 "covered businesses" with over 600 facilities requiring registration in CITSS to report their emissions. By next year, these businesses have three options: reduce their CO_2 emissions, purchase credits ("allowances" or "offsets"), or pay significant fines. Herein lies the difference between the Winners and the Losers in the world of Cap and Trade.

In a truly amazing event, the California Air Resources Board (CARB) held their first "Cap & Trade" auction on Nov 14, 2012, where businesses could purchase CO_2 allowances. In essence, these auctions are the sale of indulgences, allowing businesses to purchase units of emissions in order to avoid fines at a later date. What is so noteworthy is that $233 million of these allowances were sold in a single day. Businesses ponied up nearly a quarter of a billion dollars in one day because they believed that paying money to CARB was their best option. With four scheduled auctions each year, there will be nearly $1 billion dollars conveyed in this new "Cap & Trade" process to the State of California. However, it is through the private version of this process that the real winners will emerge.

Of the three options available, no business ("covered entity") would ever intentionally pay the "stringent penalties" (fines), as CARB's website states that willful violations can climb to $1 million per day. Rather, the businesses will purchase these "allowances" and "offsets" annually, year after year. They will become slaves to purchasing their indulgences.

The rules that allow for Winners and Losers occur through the credits that can be traded either at the CARB auctions as "allowances" or between private parties as "offsets". In order to win in this game, a business should never buy CO_2 credits. But it should always work to sell them.

Let's use an example of a manufacturing company that is generating 100,000 MTCO$_2$e with a mandated reduction of 20%. At the current auction price of $15.60, their annual cost is $312,000. Next year they will need to do this again, as an allowance is issued only for a single-use emission. And with any supply and demand commodity, as the Caps tighten, the demand on the Trades will increase.

The Winners will be the businesses that implement a sustainability program and reduce their CO$_2$ emissions *beyond* what is regulated. A comprehensive sustainability program can successfully reduce energy usage by 25-40% and reduce the carbon footprint by 70%, all with an attractive ROR. It's not about hugging the trees, it's about increasing the profits and growing the business. The key to doing this is *implementing* a sustainability *program* instead of just *executing* sustainability *projects*. Smart company leaders already know this. The others will figure it out too late. But the real winners will be the ones with enough vision to set goals *well beyond* the AB32 requirements, and then *monetize* the reductions. Yes, *monetize* the reductions. That's the key to winning. They will sell the reductions as offset credits to other businesses in California to create a new revenue stream for themselves. Once they understand how to use this new revenue stream as part of the financials in their own sustainability *program*, the revenues will be used to fund additional projects, creating even more revenue streams. These businesses will quickly learn that by executing a successful *program* once, they can create recurring CO$_2$ offsets that can be monetized year after year. The Losers will stand in line to buy these offsets, and once the game gets going, it will be too late for them to do much of anything else. The Winners will be all too happy to sell them their salvation. Legislation and Regulations come and go, but "Saving Money never goes out of Style". The businesses that choose this strategy are the real Winners. And you can take that to the bank.

Op-Ed, Pacific Coast Business Times
May, 2013

PART I: Understanding the Law

The Basics of AB32

In 2006, the state of California passed Assembly Bill 32, under Governor Arnold Schwarzenegger, titled the "Global Warming Solutions Act."

Once this law was passed, the California Air Resource Board (CARB) was directed to set up a "Scoping Plan", which detailed how to achieve AB32's goals through Regulations and Market Mechanisms. The AB32 legislation itself was fairly straightforward. But in order to enforce and fairly administer the law, a great deal more work was required to determine the finer details. As with many laws, some of the most important details are in these regulations and market mechanisms.

With any "baseline or reduction legislation," the starting and ending points of the reduction must be clearly established. For AB32, state-level GHG (Green House Gas) emissions from 1990 are used as the base for the 2020 final goals. The requirement is to return to the 1990 base by the year 2020. As a numerical measurement, the 2020 final approval limit is 427 Million Metric Tonnes of CO_2 Equivalents (MMTCO$_2$e). CARB has done an excellent job of establishing clear, measurable goals. These 1990 and 2020 dates, coupled with the resulting 427 MMTCO$_2$e numerical end goal, have essentially established the field markers, sidelines, and end-zone markers for both the players and the referees.

In 2007, CARB adopted a regulation requiring the "Largest Industrial Sources" to report and verify their greenhouse gas emissions. Their definition created a cut-off point where some California businesses were required to participate, while others were not. Over time, businesses that are operating close to the established cut-off point may cross the line as their businesses grow. Or, they may be included into the system as future regulations determine who will need to participate and comply with AB32.

CARB then identified and adopted 9 "discreet early action measures" that could be enforceable by Jan 1, 2010. These included landfill regulations, motor vehicle fuels, automobile refrigerants, tire pressures, port operations, and others.

From there, CARB adopted a "Market-Based Declining Annual Aggregate" (MBDAA) as the new "Cap & Trade". The Cap & Trade would cover major sources of CO_2e such as refineries, power plants, industrial facilities, etc. The "Cap" level will reduce over time, ultimately driving the reduction through 2020. During this period, the state will distribute (sell) "allowances", which are "tradable permits," making up the "Trade" part of Cap & Trade.

The starting and ending points have now been established, the dates have now been set, the businesses required to participate and comply have been identified, and the framework for the state's Cap & Trade have been established. Now that we have this framework, we can begin to explore the important details of this legislation.

An allowance is defined as a tradable permit to emit 1 metric tonne of CO_2e. To be clear, it can only be used once. In order to emit 1 tonne CO_2e every year, an additional allowance must be purchased for each year.

As the regulations and market mechanisms began to quickly grow and expand, some additional support was required. A new committee was convened to advise CARB on the Cap & Trade measures and is called the Environmental Justice Advisory Committee (EJAC). An additional Committee was appointed as the Economic and Technology Advancement and Advisory Committee (ETAAC).

It's important to understand how the 427 $MMTCO_2e$ was established. Many people have a tough time comprehending exactly what a tonne of CO_2 really is. Further, we are using the measure from 1990, nearly 14 years ago. It is worth noting that as EJAC and ETAAC supported CARB, they realized that some of the reductions in CO_2e were already underway, without being driven by AB32. This was due to the fact that other legislation, both State and Federal, was driving reductions in GHGs. In other words, several laws were now in place to reduce the same CO_2e. So in order to achieve the reduction back to the 1990 level, CARB acknowledged that the efforts already underway needed to be estimated and accounted for.

The initial 2020 GHG projections were for 596 $MMTCO_2e$ statewide. However, CARB established that there was a "Severe and Prolonged Economic Turndown," which would need to be accounted for. This is a very important event to understand. Since businesses in California were suffering, and the economic outlook was projected to be "severe and prolonged," the 2020 GHG projections were recalculated to 545 $MMTCO_2e$. This is an amazing disclosure in and of itself! CARB was stating that their 2020 GHG projections would need to be lowered because businesses in California were struggling. A struggling business has less growth, and less growth for a manufacturing business means less production, less energy consumed, and less CO_2e generated. This "severe and prolonged economic turndown" actually eased the 2020 goals.

But this was just the first adjustment to be made. From there, two additional measures were introduced:

a. Pavley (1) (named after Fran Pavley)
b. Renewable Portfolio Standards (RPS)

These two additional measures further reduced the 2020 estimates to 507 $MMTCO_2e$.

Pavely (1) anticipated a reduction of 31.7 $MMTCO_2e$, primarily through a 27.7 $MMTCO_2e$ reduction due to "advanced clean cars". This was effort that was already underway, as automobile manufacturers were mandated to increase fuel economy via Company Average Fuel Economy (CAFE) standards and others. The estimated 27.7 $MMTCO_2e$ was attributed to these improving fuel economy numbers in conjunction with new car sales in the state.

The other major impact to the 2020 CO_2e goals came via the Renewable Portfolio Standards (RPS). This analysis predicted a reduction of 7.9 $MMTCO_2e$ through the legislation already mandating a CO_2 reduction via the California Public Utilities Commission (CPUC).

Essentially, once AB32 was passed, the 2020 projected levels were significantly reduced! Here's a recap:

Initial 2020 CO2e Projection:	596 $MMTCO_2e$
1990 Baseline:	-427 $MMTCO_2e$
Required Reduction via AB32:	169 $MMTCO_2e$

Then,

Required Reduction via AB32:	169 $MMTCO_2e$
Severe & Prolonged Economy:	-51 $MMTCO_2e$
Pavely (1) Reduction (Anticipated):	-32 $MMTCO_2e$
RPS Reduction (Anticipated):	-8 $MMTCO_2e$
Remaining	78 $MMTCO_2e$

When AB32 was first passed, it was expected to reduce CO_2e by 169 $MMTCO_2e$. However, with other regulations already in place, as well as a suffering economy, AB32 will independently reduce CO_2e emissions by only 78-80 $MMTCO_2e$. These numbers are, of course, subject to change.

With the goals and dates set into motion, the next step was to establish how to pass carbon credits from the state to private companies. CARB determined that quarterly auctions would be the best way for this to happen. These quarterly auctions would be used to sell the allowances to California companies that were "covered entities". The first auction was held in November 2012. At the February 2013 auction, the clearing price was $13.62 and a total of 12,924,822 allowances ($MTCO_2e$) were sold during that single event.

In the "Buying Offsets and Selling Offsets" section of this book, the focus will be on the strategies of buying and selling these offsets. But prior to that, it is useful to have the background on how the logistics of allowances (different from credits) work within a CARB auction. The differences between allowances and credits will be discussed in later sections in much greater detail.

The auctions are scheduled to occur quarterly. In order to participate in an auction, it is strongly recommended that the interested parties participate in the "Auction Bidders Conference and Participant Training Webinar" (ABCPTW).

All auction notices are posted on the CARB website, and these are posted 60 days in advance. The notices communicate the number of allowances that will be offered, along with the reserve price. In a Cap & Trade (Supply & Demand) world, it should be expected that the reserve prices will increase in the future years as the caps decrease the supply of trades (allowances).

60 days prior	Notices out
30 days prior	Applications close

Thirty days prior to the auction, the applications close, giving both the participant and CARB sufficient time to prepare for the auction.

Companies that participate in the auctions must have an Auction Platform Account (APA), and designate a Primary Account Representative (PAR) and/or an Alternative Account Representative (AAR). Furthermore, the "Intent to Bid" must be submitted within the required 30-day window.

Due to the nature of the quarterly auctions, CARB requires that all participants that "intend to bid" be proven to be able to do so financially. The participant must submit a "Bid Guarantee" that is high enough to cover the expected bids. Since the "Bid Guarantee" must be able to cover the total cost of the bid (allowance bid price multiplied by the number of allowances) it must be high enough to cover the maximum allowances that the participant wants at the highest price that they would be willing to pay. If the prices increase above the anticipated selling price, the participant would need to reduce the number of allowances that they could purchase in order to remain within the "Bid Guarantee" that they established.

If the secured payment was not spent, it would be returned by the state within 12 days.

In addition, "Holding Limits" were established in order to limit the maximum allowances to be held by a participant. The maximum limit is provided to the Auction Administrator to prevent any participant from hoarding allowances.

Once the Auction begins, the bids can be rejected by the Auction Administrator if they are:

> Below the reserve
> Beyond the bid guarantee
> Beyond the bid limits
> Not allowed

It should be noted that bids are *not* rejected based on the bid price, once the reserve is met. Once the reserve is met, and bidding is underway, the auction administrator simply insures that the bidders operate within the rules established for the auction.

A "Market Monitor" was established to report the proper and accurate results of each of the auctions. The market monitor watches and observes the auction, and then summarizes and publishes the results. They act as the official auction news reporter. After each auction they provide a publicly available report detailing the auction results, statistics, participants, and details.

Once the auction has ended, the participants must complete their payment to the State of California. This process is very strict, and payments to the State of California must be in cash (wire transfer) within 7 days. The state does not allow or accept bank checks, cashiers checks, or company checks.

Once the allowances are purchased, they have a "Vintage Year." Since we are in California, this terminology makes a lot of sense, so think in terms of wine. A bottle of wine is from a specific year, or vintage, and then it can be drunk from that time forward. It can obviously not be drunk prior to its Vintage Year. The purchased allowances are the same way. They have a "Vintage Year" and they are only good from the "Vintage Year" forward. They cannot be used prior to the vintage year. At first this might seem overly complicated, but it is actually a very important facet to understand.

When you buy wine, you typically buy the wine at or after the vintage year. So you can literally drink it anytime you want after your purchase. But there are some people who might buy wine futures, and actually purchase the wine of a future vintage before the grapes are grown or harvested. This speculative buying is sometimes used to hedge against a limited supply. But obviously, if a 2016 vintage is purchased in

2014, it cannot be drunk until at least 2016. From 2016 forward, it can be drunk in any subsequent year.

This is the same concept with the vintage years of allowances. When these become available at the quarterly auctions, they can be bid on and purchased. But they cannot be used until their vintage year.

Let's say that a company realizes that its sustainability plans will not show enough progress to cover their allocations in the Compliance Instrument Tracking System Service (CITSS) for the next three years. They would then send their Primary Account Representative (PAR) to the upcoming auctions to secure the proper amount of allowances. However, the company's leader is fearful that the allowances might not be available in the subsequent years, or that the demand will dramatically increase their price at the auction. So she directs her PAR to purchase allowances in advance for several future years.

CITSS is the system created for registering and reporting, and it is used to transfer the participant's data into the auction platform if they choose to participate in an auction. It is through CITSS that CARB issues the compliance obligations to each of the "covered entities."

All registered entities are eligible to participate in the auctions. That means that any covered entity that has registered in CITSS can be part of the auction. However, unless the company (covered entity) has large or multiple facilities within California, hiring a professional broker to act as the PAR could prove to be the most beneficial. The auction process is complicated, and many small or medium sized businesses might find it hard to justify the cost of training and maintaining the skills for an internal resource to be used 4 times per year (quarterly) at the very most. Professional brokers charge a fee, usually in the 2-5% range, and using a broker can be an attractive option for some companies.

Although most of the discussion to this point has focused on the quarterly Auctions held by CARB, it is crucial to remember that the private sale and transfer between parties is permitted as well. This will be discussed in much greater detail in the sections entitled "Buying Credits and Selling Credits" and "The Winners and Losers."

CARB has put a great deal of effort into controlling what they refer to as "resource shuffling." In the simplest of terms, resource shuffling refers to the movement of CO_2 outside of the state. What CARB is attempting to curb is the potentially attractive strategy of shutting down a business and then selling the CO_2 credits while moving the business to another state. Moving businesses from California to other states (Texas is currently the most popular choice) is already a sad and growing trend for California. And the passing and enforcement of AB32 will certainly further this trend, as well as discouraging new manufacturing businesses from entering the State of California. Presented with this current business exodus, coupled with the further restrictions that AB32 will place on businesses, CARB understandably developed the resource shuffling language. Businesses are still free to leave the state, but they cannot monetize their credits in the California market if they plan to open their doors in a neighboring state.

You may have begun to pick up a potential conflict of interest developing. Let's state it in the simplest of terms:

1. The state passes a law requiring a reduction in CO_2
2. If a business cannot comply, they can pay the state for CO_2 credits
3. Private businesses will compete to sell the same CO_2 credits sold by the state

4. The state puts restrictions on the CO_2 credits that private businesses can sell

Although it is clear that the sale and transfer of private CO_2 offsets should be regulated, it poses an interesting conflict of interest when the body that regulates the private sector is also competing with the private sector in the same CO_2 marketplace.

In order for a CO_2 reduction to be claimed (whether kept or sold on the open market), CARB requires that a CO_2 reduction must be "real, permanent, quantifiable, and enforceable." This is a very good thing in order to protect those who are working tirelessly to comply with the law. With any good sustainability program, it would be easy to show the baseline data, document the work that was done, and calculate the CO_2 reduction that resulted.

CARB is in charge of adopting and developing all of the "compliance offset protocols" and they will also verify the actual offset credits.

Through the implementation of AB32, the requirements for who must participate will evolve. But one thing is clear: once a business becomes a covered entity, it will always be a covered entity. It is important for businesses to understand that there are conditions that can change their status due to their own actions. They may not be required to register in CITSS as a covered entity initially, but the business itself may do something that pushes them into a category that is covered. Once this occurs, they cannot simply "back up" and undo the activity that changed their status. Once in CITSS, the business will be a covered entity ongoing.

This is a very important situation to understand. A thorough knowledge of the AB32 Compliance (CARB's "*Cap and Trade*

Regulation Instructional Guidance," Chapter 2, Sept 2012) is absolutely necessary for any business operating in California.

Let's look at a simple example to show how this could happen. Currently, a business is a covered entity if they emit more than 25,000 $MTCO_2e$/year. In this example, the ABC Company is emitting 23,000 $MTCO_2e$/year. They had a well-connected Public Relations Manager at their site who stayed in tune with AB32 as it became state law. He briefed his plant manager on the law and reassured him that they would not need to register in CITSS because of their emission levels. The plant manager was very relieved, and focused on other areas of his business. That was back in 2012. In 2014 a new plant manager took over the operation, and decided to make big steps to improve the site's profitability. The new federal healthcare laws were looming, and his taxes increased sharply. Since plant managers typically have direct control over three cost areas (people, materials, and energy), he consolidated roles to reduce his headcount. In doing so, he eliminated the role of Public Relations Manger, and added their key duties to the Human Resource Manager. Next, he aggressively sought out new production volumes in order to spread his fixed costs across a greater number of cases. This is a classic approach, and a very effective one. He started by reducing his actual cost through reducing his headcount, and then he reduced his cost per unit of product by increasing his volume. This worked wonderfully and he was enjoying the success of his efforts.

Unfortunately, as he increased his volume, he was unaware that his emissions increased from 23,000 $MTCO_2e$ to 26,000 $MTCO_2e$. The new plant manager had "transferred in" from their plant in Missouri, where CO_2 emissions were not regulated. And without a well-informed Public Relations Manager to guide him through the AB32 regulations, he did not realize the consequences of his actions. The ABC Company is now a covered entity and must register in CITSS. Furthermore, they must now comply with all AB32 rules and regulations. While the new plant manager was once celebrating his reduced cost and improved volume, he now needs to focus on a CO_2e reduction plan in order to comply with AB32.

A very real-life issue for California businesses who are below 25,000 $MTCO_2e$ is whether or not they should grow and expand. They must weigh the cost (both dollars and resources) to become a covered entity in CITSS against the option of focusing only on cost reductions without the volume growth. For companies with facilities both inside and outside of California, it is a corporate decision that hinders California expansion and job growth. In some cases, the corporation will allocate the additional growth volume to the non-California plants and maintain the California plants at their current production levels. This hurts the viability of the California plants because they cannot lower their price per product produced and stay competitive.

If a covered entity does not comply with AB32, there are "stringent penalties" that could apply. CARB will "determine the appropriate mechanism based on the specific circumstances for a rule violation." Their ability to do this is via SB1402 (Dutton, Chapter 413, Statutes of 2010). Further details on this will be part of the discussion in the section "Penalties for Non-Compliance."

In summary, AB32 currently covers:

1. Power Generation
2. Power Importers
3. Large Manufacturing Operations

   (The current thresholds are 25,000 $MTCO_2e$)

In 2015 this will expand to full distributors. The current impact is 360 businesses touching 600 facilities, but will certainly change over time. Additional businesses will become covered entities in the years ahead and these numbers will grow. The only way that the numbers will decrease is through businesses that are currently covered entities that shut down or relocate their businesses out of the state.

The recent auction generated $233 Million in revenue for the state and the price per allowance (single use) was $15.60/MTCO$_2$e.

A partial list of Covered Entities includes:

Covered Entities

Business Sector	Threshold	Year Covered
Carbon Dioxide Suppliers	>25,000 MTCO$_2$e	2013
Cement Production	>25,000 MTCO$_2$e	2013
Co-Generation	>25,000 MTCO$_2$e	2013
Electricity – Instate generators	>25,000 MTCO$_2$e	2013
Electricity – Self generation	>25,000 MTCO$_2$e	2013
Glass Production	>25,000 MTCO$_2$e	2013
Hydrogen Production	>25,000 MTCO$_2$e	2013
Iron & Steel Production	>25,000 MTCO$_2$e	2013
Lime Manufacturing	>25,000 MTCO$_2$e	2013
Petroleum Refining	>25,000 MTCO$_2$e	2013
Pulp & Paper Manufacturing	>25,000 MTCO$_2$e	2013
Stationary Combustion	>25,000 MTCO$_2$e	2013
Suppliers of LPG	>25,000 MTCO$_2$e	2015
Suppliers of Natural Gas	>25,000 MTCO$_2$e	2015
Suppliers of RBOB /Distillate Oil	>25,000 MTCO$_2$e	2015

The Timeline of AB32

Date		Action
Sept, 2006		AB32 signed into law by Governor Schwarzenegger
Jan 25, 2007		CARB creates EJAC (Environmental Justice Advisory Committee)
Jan 25, 2007		CARB creates ETAAC (Economic and Technology Advancement Advisory Committee)
June 1, 2007		CARB adopts the List of Action Measures
Oct 25, 2007		CARB adopts the augmented List of Action Measures
Dec 6, 2007		CARB adopts the Mandatory Reporting Regulations CARB sets target for 2020 GHG emissions
Dec 12, 2008		CARB approves the AB32 Climate Change Scoping Plan
Apr 23, 2009		CARB adopts Low Carbon Fuel Standard
May 22, 2009		CARB and CA EPA creates EAAC (Economic and Allocation Advisory Committee)
Jun 25, 2009		CARB adopts the final Discreet Early Action Measure
Jan 1, 2010		All Early Action Measures take Effect
Nov, 2010		CARB holds public hearings on Cap & Trade regulations
Jan 1, 2012		All Green House Gas Rules and Market Mechanisms take effect and are legally enforceable
Dec 31, 2020		Deadline for achieving GHG emission Caps

Buying Offsets & Selling Offsets

Let's start by defining the difference between Allowances and Offsets (offset credits). In California's Cap and Trade system, an allowance and an offset are both equal to one metric tonne of carbon dioxide equivalents. Since the measurement is an impact, and not a weight, all green house gases are converted into "equivalents" to put them on an equal playing field. It's really not that complicated, as we do this in other parts of our lives every day.

Suppose I ask you to compare the value of bananas and strawberries in terms of grapes. In order to do this you need a "currency" such as dollars.

Bananas sell for $.20 per pound
Strawberries sell for $3.50 per pound
Grapes sell for $2.00 per pound

So I can write an equation for the cost of bananas relative to the cost of grapes.

$1.00 = 5 lbs bananas
$1.00 = 0.5 lbs grapes

So

5 lbs bananas = 0.5 lbs grapes

or

1 lb grapes = 10 lbs bananas

We can quickly surmise that if the currency is dollars, then grapes have a 10x factor relative to bananas. Further, if we used banana equivalents, then grapes would be 10 banana equivalents and strawberries would be 17.5 banana equivalents.

OK, I agree that this seems strange to measure things in banana equivalents, but that's how the Intergovernmental Panel on Climate Change (IPCC) determines Green House Gas (GHG) impacts with carbon dioxide equivalents (CO_2e).

Now let's look at green house gas equivalents, where the "currency" is the GWP, or Global Warming Potential. Unfortunately, the "currency" that is used to convert these gases changes over time. The GWP was established by the Intergovernmental Panel on Climate Change (IPCC), and the two most commonly used "currencies" set by the IPCC are the SAR (Second Annual Report) and AR4 (Fourth Assessment Report). For some of the most commonly discussed GHGs, the published data would appear as:

	Formula	**SAR**	**AR4**
Carbon Dioxide	CO_2	1	1
Methane	CH_4	21	25
Nitrous Oxide	N_2O	310	298

So we see that methane (CH_4) has 21 to 25 times the Global Warming Potential that CO_2 does. If an industry emits 1 metric tonne of methane, it counts as 21-25 tonnes of CO_2 equivalents, or CO_2e. For the sake of simplicity through the rest of this book, we will use the most recent 25 index for methane (CH_4) from the AR4.

So how does the SAR and AR4 relate to the Offsets and Credits?

Well, just like the bananas and grapes, these gases do not have the same value. So an allowance or offset for methane has 25 times the value of CO_2. Stop and think about that. Really. Stop and think about it.

If you have 2204 pounds (1 metric tonne) of wood chips that are sitting on your property, they will eventually decay, compost, and release methane. That's the natural process. What if you decide to burn them instead of letting them sit there and decay? Which is better for the environment? Which is better for your bottom line?

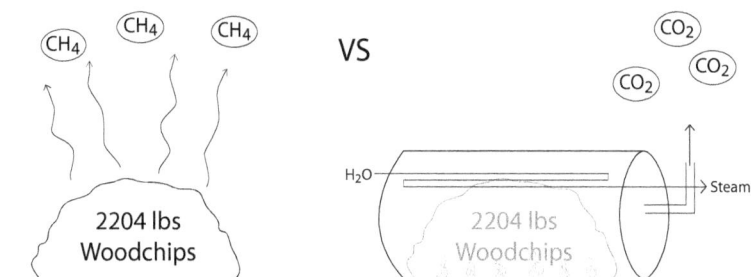

The IPCC tables indicate that if you burn the wood chips, you will give off carbon dioxide, which is bad. But if you don't burn the wood, you will give off methane, which is 25 times as bad. So here's what you do:

Burn the wood and use the heat to warm your building or make steam in your boiler. You will generate 1 $MTCO_2e$, but you will offset 24 $MTCO_2e$. You can then sell the 24 $MTCO_2e$ offsets at \$15.60/tonne and generate \$374 in revenue!

This is obviously a very simplistic example. Your wood chip pile does not make you a "covered entity" in California's AB32 (although later in the book you will read the odd way in which the forestry and logging industry is already "winning" with this new law). But it is used here to illustrate the trading impact of the GHGs with the indexes in the SAR or AR4 tables.

On the other hand, if your business is currently releasing methane, you must buy 25 $MTCO_2e$ offsets or credits for each metric tonne of methane that you want to offset.

With that background, let's get back to the difference between allowances and credits. It's really very simple:

Allowances = Traded with the state's CARB
Offset credits = Traded privately between two businesses

By this point, you should be starting to form a grin on your face. Your goal should be less focused on reducing CO_2 emissions, and more on reducing emissions with force-multipliers. Read on, and let that grin become a full smile.

Before we move on, I feel compelled to disclose my opinion on the SAR and AR4 force-multipliers:

1. *The "Rules" of the Cap & Trade "game" have been set; you cannot change them or impact them; so you might as well leverage them to your advantage*

2. *Keep this all in perspective; The IPCC is focused on reducing GHG because they believe that they negatively impact the earth's climate; they have singled out CO_2 as one of the most important GHGs, and that is why all other GHGs are indexed to CO_2. But please read this carefully:*

    CO_2 makes up 0.054% of all gases in our atmosphere

    That is not a typo. All other gases make up the remaining 99.946% of the total. This number surprises most non-technical leaders. Furthermore, only a fraction of the 0.054% is man-made CO_2. The vast majority of CO_2 in our air occurs naturally.

    Even further, Green House Gases make up only a portion of the total gases in our environment, and of those Green House gases, water vapor is by far the largest (and most important), making up nearly 95% of the total. If we eliminated ALL of the man-made CO_2, 95%+ of the Green House gases would remain unchanged.

The Winners and Losers

Nearly every time new legislation is passed, Winners and Losers emerge.

There has been a lot of discussion in the news lately regarding QE1 and QE2 (Quantitative Easing) at the Federal level of government. Quantitative Easing is the printing of more money. When the Federal government does this, there is physically more money, but it is now diluted and it is worth less. The pundits often discuss this with a contrast to the states. They claim that the Federal Government can print money, but the state governments cannot. This is not only incorrect, it is also naïve. States certainly can and do print money. It just happens in a currency that doesn't say "Federal Reserve Note" at the top.

We must keep this in mind as we take a look at this new CO_2e currency in California. CARB can sell CO_2e allowance certificates in return for cash. Make no mistake, CO_2e is a form of currency. And the State of California can "print" these.

The original Op-Ed that inspired this book was based on a premise that is still true:

- The rules that allow for Winners and Losers occur through the credits that can be traded either at the CARB auctions as "allowances" or between private parties as "offset credits"

  In order to win in this game, a business should never buy CO_2 allowances or offsets. But it should always work to sell them
- The Winners will be the businesses that implement a sustainability program and reduce their CO_2 emissions *beyond* what is regulated

- This is not about hugging the trees, it's about increasing the profits and growing the business
- The key to doing this is *implementing* a sustainability *program* instead of just *executing* sustainability *projects*
- The real Winners will be the ones with enough vision to set goals *well beyond* the AB32 requirements, and then *monetize* the reductions
- The Winners will sell the reductions as offset credits to other businesses in California to create a new revenue stream for themselves. Once they understand how to use this new revenue stream as part of the financials in their own sustainability *program*, the revenues will be used to fund additional projects, creating even more revenue streams
- The Winners learn that by executing a successful *program* once, they can create recurring CO_2 offsets that can be monetized year after year

Smart company leaders already know this. The others will figure it out too late.

Let's take a look at some real life activity to illustrate this point.

CARB has approved several categories of projects that allow carbon credits to be sold to covered entities in California. These categories include methane avoidance through anaerobic digesters, sequestration in urban and rural forestry, and the destruction of ozone depleting substances.

A new market for Winners was just created.

Timber & Logging

CARB, working with one of the nation's largest logging companies, has adopted a program that allows the logging company to sell CO_2e credits from some of their logging practices. It is not the intent of this book to argue or debate the impact of these particular logging practices. Rather, the intent is to show how that particular industry is leveraging AB32 to generate revenues.

This program with the logging company was accomplished through the maze of government and quasi-government agencies that impact the trading protocols. The Climate Action Reserve (CAR) has developed the protocols in a recommendation to CARB, who ultimately adopted the policy and created a state regulation. In the end, the timber and logging industry will be paid for the credits that their logging practices generate.

Dairy and Swine Farms

Within the category of "methane avoidance through anaerobic digesters," livestock farms are developing their new revenue streams as well. Recall that methane carries a powerful 25x factor (force-multiplier) in CO_2e, meaning that 1 tonne of methane is equal to 25 tonnes of CO_2. An average cow will generate 3.5 carbon credits. Normally, the manure from a cow would be left in the field where it would decay and produce methane. However, when utilized in a digester, this manure generates and significant supply of usable bio-gas. This has long been the case, and bio-digesters have been used throughout the country to generate this bio-gas. What has changed with AB32, however, is that there is now an additional revenue stream from these digesters. Offsetting 1 tonne of methane generates 25 tonnes of CO_2e. These can now be sold in the California market at the current market value. That equates to 1 tonne of methane generating a revenue of

$390 in credits. And that's *on top of* the revenues the digester was already seeing from the generated gas!

Interestingly, projects of these types anywhere in the USA are now eligible for the California market. So some of the real winners of AB32 may be in other parts of the country.

In both of these examples, businesses have quickly learned how to generate CO_2e credits for the California market. Financially, they are well on their way to becoming Winners in AB32.

As we have stated, a California Covered Entity has 3 choices in order to comply with AB32:

1. Reduce their CO_2e in accordance with their CITSS assignment
2. Purchase allowances from the state
3. Purchase offset credits from private businesses

Following #1 simply keeps businesses in compliance with the law. Following #2 or #3 puts them in the Loser category.

In order to be a Winner, businesses must reduce their CO_2e *beyond* what is required in CITSS and then *monetize* those gains.

Let's walk through a simple example to illustrate the potentially different outcomes for a company:

The ABC Company operates a plant in southern California and it is a profitable manufacturing facility. Through their normal operation, they generate and emit 100,000 MTCO$_2$e annually. This has been the case since the plant was built 10 years ago, and their emissions are comparable to the other plant that the ABC Company owns and operates in Kentucky. There is nothing wrong with their facility. It is a modern, well-maintained, efficient, and profitable operation. In the past, CO_2e was not a regulated emission, and it still remains unregulated at the other non-California plant. By 2015, ABC's California plant must comply with AB32 and demonstrate a 10% reduction in CO_2e emissions. Let's assume that each of the 2 plants make 10 million boxes of product each year. We will calculate the relative costs/savings over the next 5 years.

Option 1: Purchase Allowances or Offsets

ABC Company purchases 10% of 100,000 CO_2e emissions equaling 10,000 CO_2e allowances. At $15.61 per allowance, they need to purchase $156,100 in allowances. Their brokerage firm charges 3% to complete this transaction each year. As the Caps increase, the value of the "Trades" increase by 5% per year

OPTION 1 ANNUAL COST: $160,783
OPTION 1 5-YEAR COST: $888,426

Option 2: Reduce the CO_2e emissions by 10%

The ABC Company executes a Sustainability Program, which delivers a 10% reduction in CO_2e emissions. There was no net cost for the emissions reductions because the savings from the energy reduction was greater than the cost of their program.

Option 3: Reduce the CO_2e emissions by 15%

The ABC Company executes a Sustainability Program, which delivers a 15% reduction in CO_2e emissions. There was no net cost for the emissions reductions because the savings from the energy reduction was greater than the cost of their program. They monetize the 5% of CO_2e that is beyond the CITSS requirement.

OPTION 3 ANNUAL REVENUE: $80,391

OPTION 3 5-YEAR REVENUE: $444,213

So over a 5-year period, Option 3 provides $444,213 in revenue *more than* Option 2, and an impressive $1,332,639 *more than* Option 1.

That's the difference between the Winners and the Losers in AB32.

Penalties for Non-Compliance

With the options that are available to California businesses, there is no reason to intentionally enter into non-compliance.

The best option, of course, is to comply with the spirit and intent of the law, and to reduce CO_2e emissions beyond what is required in CITSS. However, if for some reason this is not possible, then there are monetary options for a business to pay their way out of non-compliance.

Purchasing allowances (from the state via auctions) or offset credits (through private parties) is a legal, and acceptable way of complying with AB32. Although it could be argued that the business has not complied with the spirit of the law, and has not done anything remarkable to improve their emissions in California, it does indeed meet the letter of the law. The business is simply purchasing some of the success of other businesses.

This approach is similar to buying indulgences, where you pay today for "sins" in the future.

Intentional violations are a very serious matter with AB32. According to CARB's website, the enforcement of AB32 is through the California Health and Safety Code 43024, which was adopted as part of SB1402. CARB has a great deal of latitude in determining penalties based on the number of offenses, the degree of the offense, and the willfulness of the offense. These violations can range from $1000/day (with no intent) up to as much as $1 million/day (willful intent).

However, there are greater, longer lasting penalties than monetary fines that can impact a business in California. And those penalties can be to the business's reputation or clients.

Here's how this situation could play out:

The Go-Go Green Company has locations in 20 states across all of the USA. They have one plant located in southern California, but their corporate headquarters is located in Houston, Texas. Their corporate leadership prides themselves on always doing the right thing, and they recently announced that they would be "20% green in 2018". It seemed doable, and it rhymed, so they announced it to their stockholders. Wall Street loved it.

Their only California plant was already struggling with profitability due to higher taxes, higher wages, and higher worker's compensation costs relative to the other plants. The action plan to reduce their emission to CITSS compliance would cost $5 million.

They decided that they did not need to spend the $5 million in California. Instead, they developed a solid plan to convert several of their plants in the mid-west to Co-Generation. It would provide a great cost savings and significantly reduce the company's carbon footprint. As a matter of fact, the entire company would show a 22% reduction in carbon footprint from the 4 Co-Gen plants installed in the Midwest. They would "go green" and save money. Wall Street loved it even more. Their 300 million shares of stock increased by $1 per share at the announcement of their strategy. The Go-Go Green Company increased its value by $300,000,000 through this strategy.

But the story does not have a happy ending. Although their strategies began to execute flawlessly, a problem started brewing on the west coast. Since the manufacturing costs were already higher in the California plant than they were in the mid west plant, the Go-Go Green Company, chose not to install Co-Gen at that site, but to simply purchase allowances to stay in compliance with AB32.

At the next CARB auction, their Primary Account Representative (PAR) purchased their allowances, and it was reported through the Market Monitor that CARB had established. Word got out. It made it to the local papers.

Why was the company that prided itself corporately for "going green" actually doing nothing in California except for buying its way into compliance? The local paper reported the facts:

- CA AB32 was passed into law and required the Go-Go Green Company to reduce it's CO_2e emissions
- The Go-Go Green Company announced a corporate strategy to reduce it's carbon footprint by 20%
- The Go-Go Company increased its value by $300 million through this announcement
- The Go-Go Company made no improvement in their California CO_2e footprint
- The Go-Go Company paid money to the State of California (in the form of allowances) to avoid paying larger fines (as a result of non-compliance)

Although this wasn't the way that the Go-Go Company would have postured the data, the local paper's article was technically correct.

This became a public relations disaster for the Go-Go Green Company. Although they complied with all prevailing laws, and did indeed reduce their corporate carbon footprint, the customers and residents in California were not happy. It got ugly. Local protests and Op-Eds in the local papers now made the national news. Corporate leadership explained that even though they were paying California for compliance allowances, they were still tracking to meet their corporate sustainability goals.

The stock dropped $2 per share. Not only did they lose the good will that they initially had, their company value dropped $600 million.

The penalties for non-compliance with the state can be significant. But the impacts to the company's reputation and relationship with the community can be far greater.

How to Win

It should be quite clear by this point that the way to win with AB32 is to exceed the required reductions in CITSS and then *monetize* the resulting credits. The monetizing of the additional CO_2e emission reductions creates a recurring revenue stream that can be used to finance other sustainability projects.

So if this is so simple in strategy, why isn't everyone doing it?

There are many reasons why more companies are not embracing this strategy. Some haven't thought about it, some don't believe that it's possible, and others simply don't know how. And sadly, some just believe it is easier to pay for their indulgences and purchase allowances from the state.

I've always found it hard to accept the excuses of why something can't be done when those around us are actually doing it. That said, let's look at these reasons that are cited above:

Some haven't thought about it

This is actually a valid reason. Most businesses focus on their core competencies to drive their businesses. As the idea of "Winning with AB32" has been shared with colleagues and associates, it has been surprising how often I've heard, "That's a good idea. I hadn't thought about that." This book has been focused on those businesses and leaders. It is focused on sharing the concept and beginning the discussion.

Some don't believe that it's possible

This is also a valid reason. But there's no reason to stay there for very long. Other businesses are winning with AB32, so it's pretty hard to argue that it's not possible. Many of those who take the position of disbelief argue that somehow their situation, their corporate policy, their technology, or their business sector make them different. They are different. Their situation is different.

But that's not true. The purpose of a business is to make money. Whether raising hogs or designing circuit boards, the purpose of a business is to make money.

The purpose of this book is to offer examples and strategies that show that it is possible, and that others are currently doing it.

Some don't know how

This is one of the most valid reasons that can be given. A leader who is honest and self-aware is invaluable. The entire second section of this book is dedicated to those leaders.

It's easier to purchase allowances from the State

This is absolutely the worst reason to give. It has Loser written all over it. Who said that this was supposed to be easy? Successful businesses never have the corporate strategy of "We always do what's easiest."

It is my sincere hope that these businesses will learn enough from this book to give up that excuse. It is the beginning of the end for that business.

PART II: Winning with the Law

Goals to Win

Winning is about achieving your goals. If you don't have goals, then you can't truly win. And if your organization has competing goals, then you're signing up for disaster.

Leaders set the goals for their organizations just as business owners set their goals for their businesses. Unfortunately, many leaders make the assumption that the goals are clear and that everyone on their team is aligned. As we will see in the Chartering process in the next chapter, goal alignment is one of the most important steps in any sustainability program.

Setting goals requires understanding and alignment. Your goals could be:

1. Reducing your energy usage
2. Reducing your purchased energy
3. Reducing your energy costs
4. Reducing your CO_2 emissions
5. Reducing your carbon footprint

These are 5 very different goals that will take you in very different directions, often competing with each other. It's key that you have clear goals and that everyone in your organization knows what they are.

Program vs Project Approach to Win

Many businesses make the mistake of *executing* Sustainability *Projects* when they really should be *implementing* a Sustainability *Program*.

Please read this again.

Many businesses make the mistake of *executing* Sustainability *Projects* when they really should be *implementing* a Sustainability *Program*.

If I were to ask a business what they have done to improve their Sustainability (Energy, CO_2, etc.), I would typically hear words in their response like:

Response A:
"we installed compact fluorescent lights...had someone do an audit... replaced equipment... upgraded equipment... installed new thermostats,

These are all tasks that they completed. This sounds like a Project Approach and they will likely realize a 15-20% improvement.

OR, I will hear

Response B:

"we staffed a leader... formed a team... employee involvement... everyone's role... collaboration... reapplication... work processes... chartered... created metrics... review process... benchmarking... training..."

This sounds like a Program Approach, and they will realize a 30-40% improvement.

If a business wants to make significant improvements, the kind that makes them Winners with AB32, they need to implement a Sustainability Program.

Let's explore this through a Q&A process:

Q. How is a "Program Approach" different from a "Project Approach"

A. With a "Project Approach" you are usually focused on a specific piece of equipment that you want to have installed. There are a lot of great Energy and Engineering Firms that offer this approach. This is also the approach that all equipment providers use.

As an example, you call a Solar Panel Company, and they install their equipment. You bought their equipment, they installed it, and now you have Solar panels.

With a "Program Approach," your leaders must understand your goals. Do you want to use less energy? Do you want to reduce your energy cost? Do you want to reduce your carbon footprint? These are 3 very different goals that can take you in very different directions. As part of the Program to meet your needs, you might install Solar Panels, or you might not. But you will develop a portfolio of options that will best meet your needs. This could include capital additions such as Heat Recovery, Solar PV, Solar CSP, Geothermal, Wind, Co-Generation, Waste Gasification, Lighting, HVAC, VSDs, VFDs, etc. Or it might focus on non-Capital areas such as load balancing, procedural improvements, cascading processes, etc.

Q. How do we know which approach is best for us?

A. If your company has the internal expertise to determine a single, specific project that you want, but you need additional resources to execute the work, then a Project Approach could be a good one.

However, if you have a sustainability or profit goal in mind (i.e.: "I want to reduce my Energy Costs by 40%"), then the Program Approach is far superior.

Q. Is there a difference in cost between the 2 approaches?

A. Yes there is.

In the short-term, a Project Approach is often the least expensive. The Firm completes their specific project, and then leaves. When you need them again, you call them again. And again. And again.

With the Program approach, you teach your resources, you invest in your people, you integrate the work into your existing organizational design and structure. You also confirm that the individual components of the Program do not compete with each other, or interfere with each other. With a Project Approach, this happens regularly.

Example: Project 1 hires a firm to install timers on their warehouse lights to reduce the kWh by 50%. Simultaneously, Project 2 hires a firm to install T8 bulbs in the warehouse to replace the T12 bulbs to reduce the kWh by 40%.

*Both are great ideas, and the contractors will certainly install the correct equipment for the Projects. But it will be the **wrong** equipment for the Program, because they are both claiming the same savings. Money and time was wasted on good ideas.*

Q. Do they both have long-term, lasting effects?

A. No, they don't.

For example: If the Utility Manager of a company decides to call an Air Compressor vendor to install a new high performance Air Compressor to save money, it will all look good in the beginning. The Compressor will perform as designed and the company will save money.

But this is one of the failures of the Project Approach. After a few years, the results will drift off, and the savings will be lost. Several factors cause this: The Utility Manager may move to another role or another company. No one else felt as though they owned the project, so the equipment is not properly maintained. Or perhaps the new equipment was never integrated into the company's maintenance program. Or worse yet, the process set-points and balance drift off, just as they did with the previous Compressor. And now you realize that you didn't really need a new Compressor, you only needed to re-balance the original one.

Q. Do I get better equipment with one approach versus the other?

A. You will almost always get better equipment and a better price with a Program Approach. The reason is simple: If you call the ABC Company to install their Widget #2, then you will pay full retail for that.

You must first evaluate if the Widget #2 is even the best equipment for you in your overall portfolio. And if it is, you must utilize your past experience and contacts to improve the competitive bidding process on the Widget #2 instead of just calling the ABC Company.

Q. Why don't all Consulting & Engineering Firms use the Program Approach?

A. Because they don't know how.

Vendors specialize in their equipment and their technology. That's why a carpenter always sees the hammer and saw as the best tools to fix the problem.

You want to leverage a firm that has manufacturing experience and has led these Programs first hand with great success. They should have personal experience with these technologies, so that you can always create the portfolio that is right for you.

High Performance Work Systems	*Heat Recovery*
Autonomous Maintenance	*PV Solar*
TPM	*Hot Water Solar*
AMS4	*CSP Solar*
PMS2	*Solar-tracking*
Skylights	*High Efficiency*
Regression Analysis	*Lighting*
Failure Analysis	*Building HVAC*
OSHA Requirements	*Waste*
Gasification	*Geothermal*
Federal & State Incentives & Rebates	*Bio-Fuels*
Monetizing Carbon Credits	
CA AB32	

Critical 12 Steps to Win

In order to win with AB32, it is critical to have a good plan. In this next section, we will explore the components of a solid plan. It's easy to say, "Reduce your CO_2e emissions so that you can monetize your gains." In practice, it is much more difficult to execute. But the winners will have a plan, and it will be complete and comprehensive.

If you are serious about pushing forward and winning, there are a series of "Energy Elements" that will guide you through the process. These 12 key steps will establish the framework for reducing your CO_2e emissions through energy conservation.

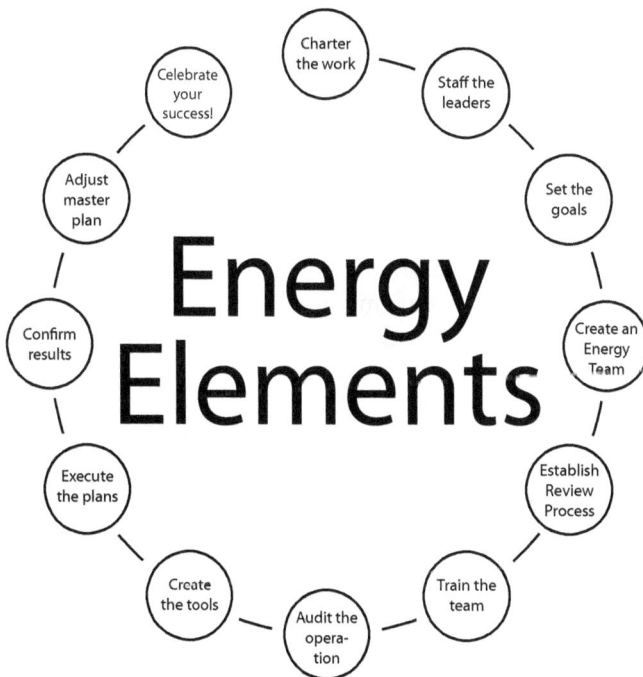

Charter the Work

Chartering the work is one of the most important steps in establishing an Energy Program, which is why it is listed first. Unfortunately, it is also the step that is most often skipped. Chartering the work is an especially critical step for large organizations or companies where there are competing resources. It would be fair to say that most Energy Programs fail because they were not properly chartered.

Chartering occurs when a senior leader in the organization documents on paper what the goals are for the team to deliver. The charter must contain the goals, the resources that will be made available (both people and money), who will lead the team, and who will sponsor the team.

The chartering process is actually quite difficult because there is ambiguity in what most leaders request. The chartering process is a commitment between the senior leader and the team, and it drives out that ambiguity.

Let's use an example:

Bob Jones, the VP of Engineering at the FrozenPop Company staffs a new role called the "Energy Program Director". He tells the new leader, Amy Parkinson, that her goal is to reduce their energy usage. She immediately goes to work.

I can guarantee that this will end badly. Here are some of the reasons why:

1. They have not established a metric
2. They have not defined the base
3. They have not established a budget
4. They have not established her team (her resources)
5. They have not established a timeline
6. They have not clarified the goal

7. They have not established a review process

So let's play this out in the following narrative to see why it was destined to end badly:

Amy was a great leader. She was well liked in the company, and had a long history of successful assignments. She liked Bob, and was excited to work directly for him. She had lots of ideas to reduce their energy usage. Bob was also a strong and well-liked leader. He was very pleased to have Amy on his team and knew that they would get along very well together on this work. Because of their successes and trust in each other, they decided to breeze through the chartering process and start executing their ideas. But they skipped so many steps in the chartering process that they didn't realize that they didn't have alignment on how to measure their success. And even worse, they had not clarified their goal. Bob stated that he wanted to "reduce their energy usage," and this is what Amy went off to do. But what Bob _really_ meant was that he wanted to "reduce their energy _cost._"

Here's what happened:

Amy started the project in January, in a plant that was located in northern Pennsylvania. As the winter turned to spring and spring to summer, the cost to heat their 2 million square foot warehouse steadily dropped. Amy was happy because the energy usage went down. She pulled together her team and began executing a number of independent energy projects. They installed solar panels on their facility's roof, lowered the thermostats in the offices, put motion sensors on the light switches, and installed a lot of LED lights. She felt as though these were all the right things to do, and spent about $2 million in capital to install the new equipment. In June the company launched a new FrozenPop flavor for the summer, and it did not do well in the market. Sales dropped drastically, and half of their lines were shut down to idle. As a result, their energy usage dropped dramatically (making less product required less energy). In the VP's mind, he was hoping for a 20% reduction in energy costs, but he never actually wrote that into the charter. Bob had worked with Amy before, and he figured that she probably knew that's what he wanted. In the July cost review Bob's finance leader told him that there has been a 35% reduction in energy cost since January. The VP was thrilled that Amy had far surpassed the 20% goal that he had, and assumed that the energy team could now "coast" for the rest of the year. Unfortunately, they had not set up a formal review process as they chartered the program, so Amy was not a part of the finance reviews. She was not present at the review. As a result, she was unable to share her perspective on their actual progress and results.

FrozenPop's sales were still down, so Bob pulled resources from the energy team and reassigned them to the product improvement team. The team quickly revised their flavoring, and by August, sales were up by 50% (making more product and requiring more energy). By October, the weather had cooled dramatically, and the heating costs for the warehouses increased sharply. By the time the February cost review occurred, the finance leader reported that their energy costs were 70% higher than they were 6 months ago in July. The VP saw Amy as a failure and summoned her to explain what she was doing.

So what happened?

By failing to establish the correct metrics, such as an ECI (Energy Consumption Index), seasonal impacts and product swings caused the energy costs to cycle wildly. Amy did not have the proper metrics established to show the impact of her work. In addition, the energy trends were misleading, and the VP incorrectly shifted resources within his organization to where he thought that they were most needed. Furthermore, the results were compared to the previous month instead of being compared to the same month the previous year. This was the worst mistake of all. Many products (such as FrozenPop treats) have seasonal trends, and many facilities (like those in northern areas) have seasonal weather that impacts their energy costs significantly.

What should have happened?

In the chartering process Amy should have worked with the VP to establish clear, measurable results:

a. 20% ECI reduction, where ECI is defined as:

$$ECI = \frac{(mmbtu/product\ unit)}{(mmbtu/product)\ YAG}$$

b. The 20% goal must be achieved within 24 months
c. A budget of $2 million will be available, but the capital must deliver a 25% IRR

The Energy Consumption Index (ECI) measures the amount of energy (mmbtu) that is required to make a unit of product divided by the energy per the same unit of product a year ago (YAG). The product seasonality and the weather seasonality are neutralized in this measure. Furthermore, if organic (non-seasonal) sales increase or decrease, they are generally neutralized as well, since the ECI metric is on a per production unit basis.

ECI is unit-less. All of the units cancel out, leaving only an index. So a 0.8 ECI indicates a 20% reduction. A 0.75 ECI indicates a 25% reduction, etc.

One of the sad truths in any organization is that even good people often skew the data in a way that places them in a favorable light. The ECI is pretty resistant to that, as there are no complicated calculations to perform. The purchased energy is recorded from the energy bill and it is divided by the amount of product that was produced. There's really no way to "fudge" the numbers.

ECI Chart
Base Year + 3 Actual Years

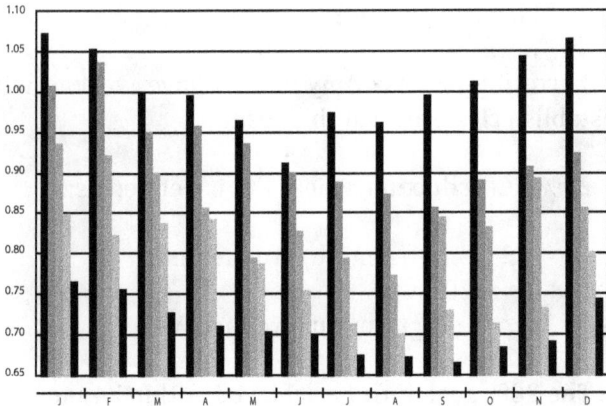

Decrease in ECI and Increase in Green Fuels

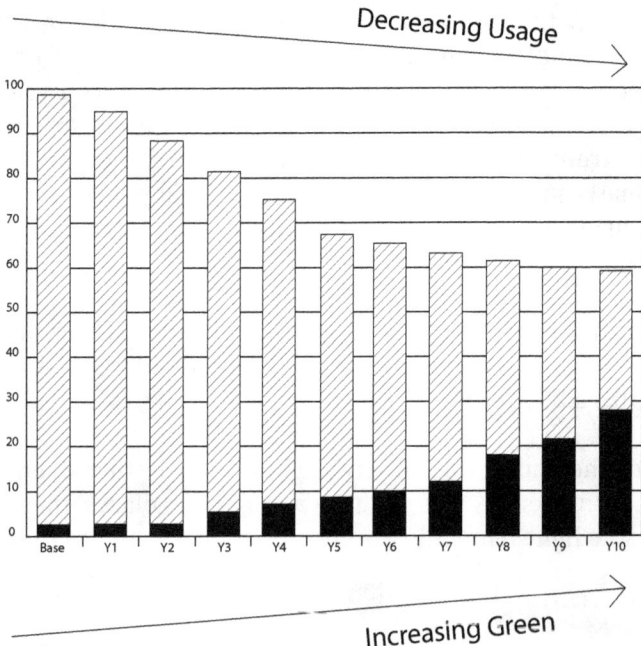

Finally, you can cater the ECI to your energy use. Industries heavily dependent on natural gas could use mmbtu/unit or mcf/unit or therms/unit, while industries heavily dependent of electricity could use kWh/unit. The ECIs can still be compared with each other because the units all drop out.

One of the final pitfalls that wasn't fixed in this example was the actual goal itself. Amy was told to "reduce their energy usage". Was that even the right goal? Shouldn't their goal have been to reduce their energy _cost_?

In the real world there are extraordinary projects executed where energy _usage_ was _increased_ in order to _reduce_ energy _cost._ But in order to do this successfully, the charter must be very specific about the required goal. See the section on "Fuel switching " in the next chapter to see how this can be done.

In this example, Amy also made a critical flaw by choosing to install solar panels. She did this because she thought that it sounded like a good idea and she knew of other companies that had done the same. Bob didn't question it because he assumed that Amy had thoroughly studied it.

Let's study why solar panels were wrong:

First, if Bob's stated goal of "reduce energy usage" was followed, solar panels would never accomplish this. Inside the factory, the pumps, motors, chillers, and lights would all use exactly the same amount of electricity. Solar panels will _never_ reduce your energy usage. They simply can't. They will reduce your _purchased_ energy, but they will not reduce your energy usage. So the project had no chance of supporting Bob's deployed goal.

Secondly, if Amy's goal of "reducing energy costs" was followed, solar panels would never accomplish this in the 2-year time line. Even though solar panel technology has increased dramatically over the years, it still does not offer anything near a 2-year return on investment. As a result, FrozenPop's costs would have increased for those 2 years.

Setting goals requires understanding and alignment. Your goals could be:

1. Reducing your energy usage
2. Reducing your purchased energy
3. Reducing your energy costs
4. Reducing your CO_2 emissions
5. Reducing your carbon footprint

These are 5 very different goals that will take you in very different directions, often competing with each other. It's key that you have clear goals and that everyone in your organization knows what they are.

Staff the Leaders

The selection of the Leader for the Energy Program is a critically important step, and must be completed with a great deal of thought and consideration.

One of the main considerations is to select an autonomous leader who will have sufficient time to develop the necessary structure, tracking systems, and masterplans to deliver against the sustainability goals that were deployed to them.

You must invest in your Leader to develop expertise. In some cases this will be the first creation of an Energy/Sustainability Team for your business. So it will be important to build expertise in your Energy Leader as your program moves forward. Although some of this will happen naturally due to the nature of the work, this growth will be much more effective and efficient if it is legitimized via the Leader's Work

Plan and Reward System. Having the time allocated to simply "explore, benchmark, and learn" will allow the Energy Leader to keep a healthy vision of what's available outside of their plant.

It's easier to lead with passion and convert skeptics when armed with the real life examples of someone else's accomplishments. So having first hand data can be invaluable when discussing the merits of solar panels, geothermal heating, condensate return efficiencies of 95%, converting pressure into electricity, balancing compressed air systems, or delivering huge savings through Energy Promotions. Nothing beats seeing someone else already doing it successfully.

The Leader must also be very "hands-on" with their approach to the work. This is not work that can be done from behind a desk.

The Energy Leader must be able to tour the operation, audit the systems, and find defects. They must be able to understand the technology of their processes. And they must be able to rally people to achieve some staggering goals. They must also be able to communicate effectively with all levels of the organization.

Set the Goals

An Energy Conservation Program must include clear metrics that capture exactly what is set as the Goal – Conservation. Although there is not any single perfect measure, there are certainly a lot of bad ones. Measures that are impacted significantly by pricing, sourcing, or volume will all create huge distractions to the team that is trying to improve their conservation and measure their results. In most cases, pricing or healthy volume growth could overshadow the results of the conservation. That is not to say that the work will not deliver significant savings. Rather, it means that the results will become difficult to quantify unless the correct metrics are used so that these other factors are accounted for.

On the other hand, any metric that does not capture the impacts of initiatives, new equipment, or fuel play strategies will only reveal a portion of the conservation efforts, and misleads the leaders who are responsible for evaluating the results.

As discussed earlier, the ECI (Energy Consumptive Index) is a very good measure of an Energy Program. It is an index to a selected base, and captures all of the right things without being impacted by pricing or volume growth. It is simple and fairly pure.

With this measure, a "base" year is selected. The entire 12-month period should be used to capture any seasonal cycling or impacts. Once this is established, the ECI always refers back to that particular base that was set for the ECI.

The MMBTUs are taken directly from the utility invoices and the amount of product produced is provided by the finance group. That way there is no room for inconsistencies or adjustments to the ECI numbers. It is a fairly straightforward metric.

As progress is made, the ECI will decrease. For example, if the site's conservation efforts have improved to the point where they have reduced their energy need 5% to produce the same case, then their ECI would be a 0.95. At any point in time the ECI provides an immediate measure of the conservation improvement.

A further benefit of the ECI is that each site is indexed to itself. So if the different sites have different production SKUs, generations of equipment or technologies, etc., these are all nullified.

There are a few potential watch outs with this measure:

1. ECI is a measure of improvement, not absolute performance. In a Program with multiple sites, the site with the best ECI will be the Site with the best *improvement* from its base. But that site could still have the worst absolute mmbtu/product. As a matter of fact, the sites with the best performance (mmbtu/product) could actually have the weakest ECI because they are already the benchmark and don't have as much opportunity as some of the other sites. That's not to say that they can't also improve. It's just that their rate of improvement might be slightly slower than sites with bigger opportunities.

2. Changes in "interplants" may need to be adjusted if the interplants are "in-process" materials. In some businesses, for example, over 90% of the energy associated with making a case of product occurs in the process operation. If sub components are interplanted to another site and converted into product cases, the receiving site enjoys producing those stats with only the remaining 10% energy demand, while the sending site receives no "product credit" from the sub components that they produced. In this example, an adjustment may be in order. Keep in mind, however, that if these interplants are consistent with those that occurred in the base, no adjustments would be necessary.

3. ECI cannot be converted directly into savings. This is because it intentionally does not capture pricing impacts. If a site is showing an ECI = .85, for example, they have reduced their energy usage per stat by a healthy 15%. If commodity prices increased by 15%

over that same time, then the net savings would be zero. However, if the conservation efforts had not been completed, the energy costs would have increased by 15%. A detailed scorecard can display both of these fairly easily.

Following is an ECI graph for a company that operates several facilities across the country. What is important to note is the seasonal impacts of the ECI due to the location of some of those plants. Although reporting a YTD ECI will smooth out these curves somewhat, it is important to see the indexed improvements from year to year.

Annual Energy Trends
ECI

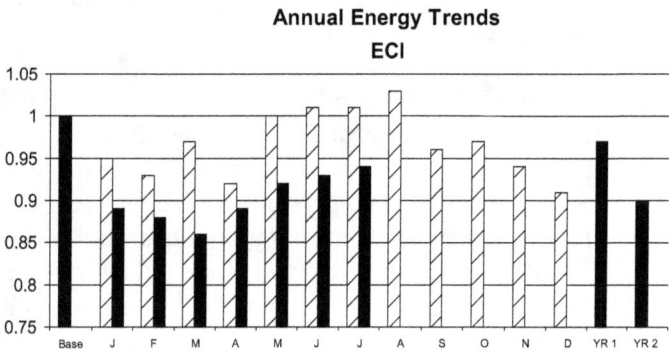

It is easy to see from the first bar that the base is defined as an ECI = 1.0. The seasonal winter impacts of Year 1 show that even though the year averaged an ECI = 0.97, there was a swing from the low summer months to a high through the winter monthts. Year 2 follows the same seasonal impact, but shows the improvement over the previous year, capturing seasonal weather and seaonal sales.

Create the Team

Total Employee Involvement (TEI) must be the cornerstone to the Strategy.

This means that 100% of your employees must be engaged.

While there is a temptation to depend on external firms or consultants to audit your facilities and to generate project lists that are often capital-intensive, this approach will likely have two significant disadvantages:

1. Only a fraction of the total opportunities that are available will be realized.

2. Very little Savings will occur in the first 12 months. This is not complicated, but it is often overlooked.

The best way to find losses is to teach the people who operate the equipment every day. Outsiders can look for general losses, but will find only a small portion of what is really there. The key, then, is to teach your teams and employees how to become human sensors and identify these losses on their own. This will be the key to finding and fixing defects quickly.

Secondly, capital projects take time. There are engineering studies, financial evaluations, peer reviews, funding, procurement, delivery, installation, etc. It is likely, then, that this approach will provide little to no real savings in the first 6-12 months of the effort. On the other hand, a year-one plan of "returning to base" through TEI will return immediate savings. As a simple example, if you patch a leaking compressed air fitting today, you don't have to wait. You will see the electrical savings on the compressor the very next day.

You should employ a Pyramid Strategy

In any well-designed Energy Program there will never be a lack of ideas. Many will be good, some will not be good, and several will border on ridiculous. However, what will be common in nearly every location is a desire to focus on the new, innovative technology. This is healthy, but not very helpful. At the beginning of the Program you want very few, if any, resources focused on new, breakthrough technologies. Not only are they slower to deliver savings, but the expertise required to evaluate these technologies is too costly to develop in large numbers of people. Rather, the foundation of the Program must focus on "Fixing and Restoring." This should be what 90% of the resources focus on during the first 1-2 years. This will provide immediate savings, establish credibility for the approach, and create momentum for future ideas to build from. It will also maximize the benefits of everything done subsequently. You would never install a new supercharger on an engine that has clogged valves and cracked sparkplugs. You would fix those first.

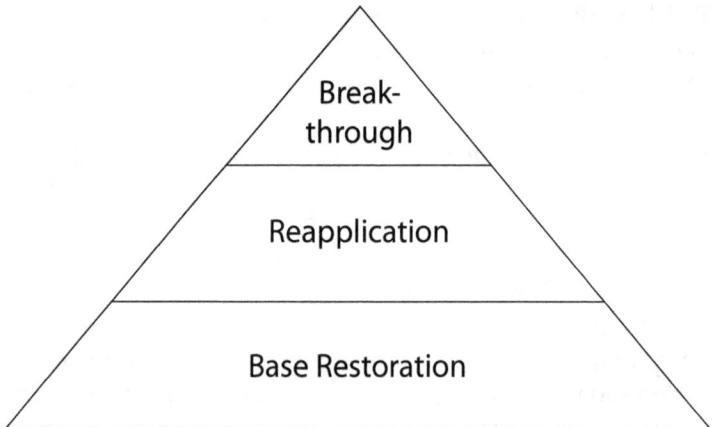

The "Fix and Restore" phase has many of the components of autonomous maintenance. But it must also include a number of improvement projects. The base must be healthy, focusing on fixing leaks and repairing defects. However, it must also include small improvement projects to balance usage profiles, adjust loads, optimize operating procedures, and stabilize the operation.

The next phase is to "Reapply Existing Technology" and will likely overlap considerably with the "Fix and Restore" phase. But it will likely be with different resources and at different locations. A good approach is to determine your internal benchmarks and have the benchmark site move into the "Reapply Existing Technology" phase as the remaining sites all focus on closing the gap to the benchmark. As you measure your operations, and identify the best in each of the operational sub-units, you will be amazed at how well different departments in your organization are operating already.

As an example, let's break a typical manufacturing operation into 4 sub-units. The efficiency data may appear something like this:

	Sub 1	Sub 2	Sub 3	Sub 4	
Plant 1	[85%]	[85%]	[85%]	[85%]	= 52% Overall
Plant 2	[92%]	[79%]	[84%]	[85%]	= 52% Overall
Plant 3	[79%]	[92%]	[80%]	[89%]	= 52% Overall

Each plant's overall efficiency is simply the product (multiplication) of each sub-unit with each of the other sub-units in that particular plant. In this scenario, it would be easy to just look at the overall plant efficiency, and believe that all 3 plants are running the same. However, if we took the best performance in each of the operations, we would see that the true capability is actually much greater than the 52% efficiency.

True Capability   [92%] [92%] [85%] [89%] = 64%
Overall

This exercise demonstrates that this company has already demonstrated that they could operate at 64% overall efficiency, even though each of their individual plants are performing at 52% overall efficiency. By simply using the best efficiency in each of the 4 sub-units, an efficiency of the true capability can be determined.

Although an entire book could be written on benchmarking sub-units in order to increase the efficiency of the whole, we will simply point out that this is the intent behind the middle of the pyramid. Reapplying the best of each sub-unit to the other plants will generate a great deal of savings to your program.

The top of the Pyramid is "New Technology." This is fun and exciting stuff that almost everyone wants to go work on. But the reality is that this should be led by a few people in only very specific locations. New technologies must be evaluated, tested, and then checked to insure that they are "fit for use." Although much of this work may occur with discreet resources in parallel with the other two phases, it should be largely transparent. The real key to the timing on this is to have the technologies ready to apply once the sites have achieved local benchmarks and are ready for more. Each site must "earn the right" to move to a higher place in the pyramid. This includes implementing the proper systems to prevent erosion at any level of the pyramid as they move upwards. Many sites fall into the trap of ignoring their base restoration as they move towards the top, only to realize that the new gains in the latter phases are masked by their eroding base restoration. The gains must always be systematized before moving on.

Establish the Reviews

Winners always keep score. And they know how important it is to do it in a way that is fair and consistent. Don't lose that point. It must be done fairly and consistently. Although this seems like common sense, it is rarely done correctly outside of the text book.

Let's go to another site at the ABC Company. Katy Waterman has been leading the company's energy team, and they have had some very solid results. They are using the ECI metric to track their progress, so there should be no confusion about the progress that they have made. Katy is looking forward to reviewing the results with the team's sponsor, Sheldon Boone, and she has invited the entire team to participate to share in the credit at the review.

Katy kicks off the meeting with the graph that shows a 15% improvement in results year to date versus a goal of 10%. Her ECI has improved from a 1.00 to an impressive 0.85. She covers the status of the projects and efforts to increase total employee involvement, and then she looks to her sponsor for approval and recognition.

Sheldon shows a small smile and tells her that the results look fine. But he then proceeds to tell Katy that she should not be too happy about her results because it was an "easy" month for her team. He explained that he staffed the two open positions on the team, and that the production plant had run smoother than normal. That created fewer distractions for the team and made their gains easier than they might have been otherwise. In closing, Sheldon reminded the team that the same month the previous year had very poor results, so it was "easy" to make this month look good.

Sheldon made a fatal flaw. He changed the rules. He thought that he was being a good leader. He believed that good leaders always pushed hard and asked for more. But he did that in the wrong place. A good leader increases the expectations in the goal-setting process, not in the results review. Sheldon made a fatal flaw. He changed the rules. The team left the meeting deflated. Worse, they decided that their efforts were not valued and they lost motivation.

Let's explore this with a sports analogy. The Dallas Cowboys are playing the New York Giants. The Giants are on their own 5 yard line, and the quarterback blows the snap. He fumbles the ball, and a Dallas defensive player scoops up the ball on the 2 yard line and hops into the end zone. Touch down! But wait. The referee shows a small smile and tells the team that they will only get 4 points instead of 6 points. Sure, a touchdown is usually worth 6 points, but he pointed out that Dallas didn't have to work very hard to score that touchdown. After all, they only had to go 2 yards. How was that fair when earlier in the quarter New York had to move the ball 69 yards to score their touchdown? Nope, it was too "easy," and he only awarded the team 4 points.

Any football fan reading this would say, "That's crazy. You always get 6 points for a touchdown. Those are the rules!" And that fan would be correct.

So why would we ever change the rules in the business world? If a goal is met, then the goal is met. The sponsor must always play fair.

Secondly, the reviews must be consistent.

After the last review, Katy helped her team recover, and they updated their plans and delivered an even better month than the previous one. And there were a lot of production upsets and other distractions this time. Sheldon would certainly give them credit for their work this month. It was not an "easy" month by any stretch of the imagination.

It was such a difficult month that Sheldon was swamped with problem-solving meetings and personnel meetings to address the production problems. Two hours prior to his review with Katy, he had his assistant call her to cancel the meeting. He had a lot of problems to deal with this week, and he would just wait and cover their results in next month's review. Sheldon just made his second fatal flaw.

In order to keep the energy team on track and motivated, there must be clear metrics. But there must also be frequent, fair, and consistent reviews. The team should review their results weekly, and generate a gap plan for any outages or missed expectations. They should have a monthly review with their sponsor, and they should also have a quarterly or semi-annual review with their sponsor's boss in order to insure alignment.

Train the Team

In order for any team to be effective they must be trained to do their work. Each member of the team should have a personal, written training plan, developed specifically for them. Just as important, they must have time protected in their schedule to complete their training. Specifically, they should receive training in:

- The metrics, measures, and goals
  They should be able to hand-calculate any of the results that are done automatically.

- Case Studies
  They should have access to all of the case studies generated by the other leaders and the other facilities so that they can learn from the work of others and reapply the learnings to their own plant.

- Leadership
  They should be trained in general leadership skills regarding plans, forecasts, gap analysis, results tracking, results reviews, action plans, master plans, metrics, coaching others, statistical analysis, etc.

- External technology
  They should attend at least 1 external event annually. This could be an energy conference or a technology conference on a specific technology that they are exploring (such as geothermal, solar, lighting, etc.).

- Specific energy tools
  They should learn how to perform calculations and dimensional analysis. They should also know how to conduct energy tours and use technical equipment such as laser thermometers, hygrometers, anemometers, illuminometers, etc.

An investment in the individual team member's training will not only prepare them to perform at their best, but it will also send a strong message that they are valuable resources that you are investing in.

Audit the Operation

Energy audits are worthy of an entire book on their own. They are the very crux of an energy conservation program, and the appropriate approach to the energy audit must be carefully considered for each type of business.

First of all, let's stop calling these audits. Audits have bad connotations, and evoke feelings of the IRS trying to catch us doing something wrong. A much better descriptor is assessment, tour, study, or analysis. I prefer "energy tour" and will use that terminology through the rest of the book.

Let's break potential tours into the basic types of:

1. Execution (Internal or External)
2. Frequency (Periodic or Continuous)
3. Focus Area (General or Specific)

The first, and most important question, is who should perform the energy tour. Internal resources are the ones inside of your company. External resources are those that you bring in from the outside.

It is strongly recommended that you use internal resources only.

Many will argue that external resources have more expertise than internal resources in this area. While this is true, it is only transitional, and is not a good reason to use an external resource to complete your energy tours.
The problems with using external resources for these tours are many:

- Your organization will not feel that they own the defects or opportunities that are identified

- Your organization might be spiteful or defensive that an outsider made a list of how they could do better

- While external resources are good at identifying opportunities, they are less successful at implementing the solutions

- External resources don't fully understand your operation

- External resources don't fully understand your culture

- External resources don't fully understand your work processes

- External resources that offer tours for free are often trying to sell something that will (of course) be identified in the tour

- Your organization will become dependent on the external resources and view them as the "experts" rather than your own internal resources

So why do so many companies use external resources? Primarily because it is easy, there are a lot of firms that offer this service, and many internal resources don't know how to do this.

It is crucial that you have internal skills to execute energy tours. This is very important. If you do not have the skills to it internally, *then build those skills!* Don't contract it out!

This is worth repeating. If you must use external resources, hire the ones that can teach your internal resources how to execute efficient, productive energy tours. Don't hire them to do the tours. Hire them to *teach you how to do the tours* so that critical skill resides within your organization.

Create the Tools

If the energy conservation effort is new to your facility, it will be necessary to invest in creating the tools that you and your team will need.

The most important part of this step is to create the tools within your existing system. This will simplify your work processes and allow them to become part of your culture. This cannot be emphasized enough. The results tracking must integrate with your other results tracking, the budgeting and staffing processes must integrate with the existing budgeting and staffing processes, etc.

Any new, stand-alone systems have a much lower likelihood of success. Additionally, if those stand alone systems are created by external resources or consultants, they are almost certainly doomed to fail.

That said, the key tools for the program must include:

- ECI tracking tools and graphs
- Energy scorecards with ECI and financials
- Energy Masterplan
- Overall sustainability template
- Capital funding process
- Energy project tracking sheet
- Reapplication forum
- Case study template and reapplication tracking
- 3-year and 5-year energy reduction plans
- 10-year "green" Plan
- Energy tour procedures
- New member onboarding and training

A final word: Resist the temptation to have all of these tools created before you staff the roles. You will generate less ownership by deploying the tools to your team than you will by enrolling them in the development of the tools!

Execute the Plans

Most leaders don't include "execute" as a step. They typically see the "execute" as what they do to the other steps. But determining *how* to execute is absolutely crucial so that it is done correctly. For example:

- Do you assign the work or ask for volunteers?
- Do you execute with a few strong players, or do you want 100% total employee involvement?
- Do you deploy the tasks to your team or do you enroll them in determining them?
- Are the action plans generated from the "top down" or from the "bottom up"?
- Do you rely on external resources or do you develop the skills within your team?
- Do you launch across all of your facilities or start with a test site first?
- Do you focus your reward system on the carrot or the stick?

These are all important considerations. And they are much easier to implement at the beginning of the execution than they are to go back and modify later.

Confirm the Results

It is always important to confirm the results of any team. This can be difficult for many teams, as the bottom line results are often difficult to measure. There are countless examples where each of the different cost-savings teams within a plant report their savings to the plant finance manager. However, the total plant savings are actually less than the sum of all of the project team's claimed savings.

There are several reasons for this:

1. Some results degraded as others improved
2. Multiple groups claimed the same savings
3. The metrics to measure the savings were not correct, and other influences such as inflation, client requests, production volumes, seasonal impacts, shifting of fixed versus variable costs, etc., skewed the results

The good news is that energy conservation is incredibly simple and easy to measure. Because the "Set Your Goals" was completed properly, and an ECI metric has been established, confirming the results is remarkably simple. The ECI index is based on two pieces of data: the utility bill and the production volume.

Adjust the Plan

You will need to adjust your plans. There are 3 reasons why this could occur:

1. Your results could be better than you expected
2. Your results could be less than you expected
3. Your leadership changes or modifies your goals

Do not discount that #3 is a high probability. But for whatever reason, there will be a need to adjust the plan. If this is a step that is already identified on the action plan, your team will see this as a normal process and welcome the option to update the plan and provide their best input. Without scheduling this in advance in the action plan, your team will view this as a problem, likely a failure, that causes them to "fix" a "broken" plan. This would be neither helpful, nor accurate.

Plans change, and results are rarely exactly as predicted. Furthermore, leaders will tend to expect more when the results are good. Plant leadership is responsible for many teams across their site, and it is common for them over time to expect more and more from the successful teams, while expecting less and less from the unsuccessful teams. This isn't necessarily bad, but it must be recognized by the energy team's leader to avoid the pitfalls that it can create.

Celebrate Your Success!

Although it may sound a bit "lame" to schedule a celebration as a part of an action plan, it is important to do so. The truth is that most great leaders are driven by accomplishment and success. The reward for a job well done is a new, tougher job. And that is satisfying to the leader. However, real energy conservation is a *team* effort, and not everyone on the team will be rewarded with a promotion or a new assignment. So it's important to schedule the celebration in advance for two reasons. First, it communicates to the team that there will be rewards and/or recognition for their hard work and results. Secondly, it insures that the celebrations occur and don't get skipped over. In today's busy business environment, particularly in manufacturing plants, it is easy to move quickly from one success to the next challenge.

It is a common phenomenon for the personnel in a plant to want to work on the projects that have the best results and the greatest recognition. That's just human nature playing out in a manufacturing environment. As your energy conservation program gains steam and begins to deliver significant savings, there will be attention given to them by your plant leadership. Others will quickly realize this and want to be a part of the success story. Resources will flow, not so much from deployment, but from enthusiasm. Success breeds success.

When this happens, it is imperative for the team and the leader to refrain from being protective or closed to the new offers of help. Ronald Reagan was known for saying, "There is no limit to what a man can do or where he can go if he does not mind who gets the credit."

I would add to that, that there is more than enough work for everyone to contribute and be part of the celebration. My motto is that "We can always order another bottle of champagne!"

Technology to Win

We live in a world that is just spilling over with technology, and every day it seems there are new advances and new options for us to consider.

The following is a very brief list of some of my favorite technologies. Keep in mind that these should only be small projects as part of a larger energy program, but it's still good to stay abreast of what's available.

ASDs & VFDs

Adjustable frequency drives have been around for quite awhile, and they typically offer a very good return on investment.

Let's say that we have an electric motor powering a pump that is pumping a fluid to a process module. The pump can deliver 100 gpm, but the process module only requires 50 gpm. So a control valve is used to restrict the flow to the desired level. This is a very common design in facilities today.

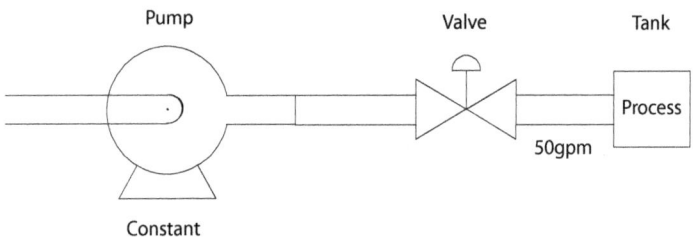

The drawback is that the 20 hp motor is always running at full capacity, and the flow is throttled back by the valve. This is similar to having your car at full throttle, and then using your brakes to slow the car down to the speed limit. You are always using the energy for full capacity, and that's not very efficient. A Variable Frequency Drive (VFD) is able to change the speed of the motor itself, and only generates the flow through the pump that is required by the process module. This is how you drive your car today (hopefully). You only depress the gas pedal for the specific power that you need at that moment. The savings can be significant.

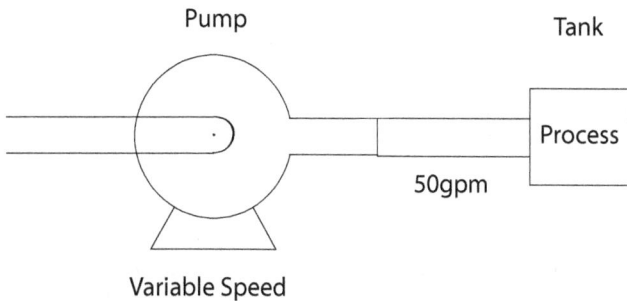

Pump   Tank

Process

50gpm

Variable Speed

Adjustable Speed Drives (ASD) include all of the available technologies that vary the speed of the drive. VFDs are a type of ASD and accomplish the task by varying the frequency of the drive. But there are other options available in addition to the VFDs.

One of the most interesting and promising technologies is the Magnetic Air Drive. It consists of a coupling with two spinning plates, one of copper and one of industrial rare-earth magnets, to manipulate the output speed. One of the real benefits of the air coupling is that there is no physical contact between the two sides of the coupling. And in high priority equipment, there is the added benefit of speed to install, as there is no need for laser alignment (or double-dial alignment) prior to start-up.

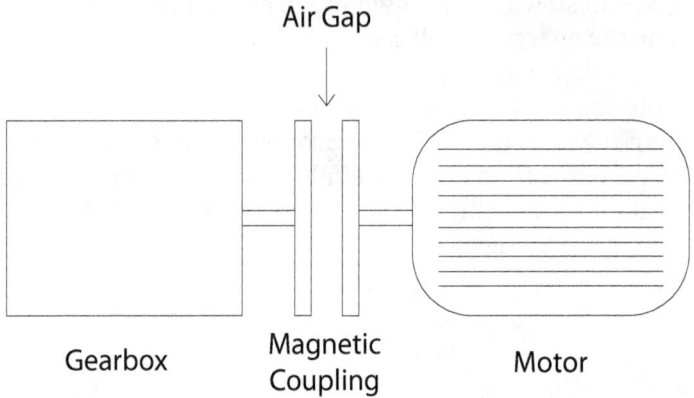

Air Gap

Gearbox   Magnetic   Motor
               Coupling

When evaluating the difference in cost (and return on investment) between the VFDs and the magnetic air drives, it is prudent to compare their 10 year life costs. While the two technologies may have very similar financials in the first 5 years, they may look dramatically different at 7 or 10 years.

While the purchase price of VFDs and magnetic drives are comparable, the magnetic drives may have up to twice the service life. So in a 5 year comparison the costs may look similar, but in the 10 year comparison, there might be 2 purchased VFDs where there is only 1 purchased magnetic air drive.

Bio-Digester Gas

Bio-Digesters are not new, dating back literally hundreds of years. But the advances in controls, monitoring, and materials have helped this technology advance quickly in recent years.

Bio-Digesters, as the name suggests, utilize a biological feedstock to generate the resulting methane gas. As a result, bio-digesting is a very simple and natural process. But the key is that the fuel must be an organic "bio fuel". In a simple agricultural example, livestock manure and switch grass are used as the feedstock. The mixture is diluted with water to achieve the optimal solids (typically about 2%), and the slurry is heated to the optimal temperature (typically about 98F). As the slurry of bio-mass "cooks", methane is slowly released. The methane gas can then be used for any number of purposes, from firing a boiler to generating electricity.

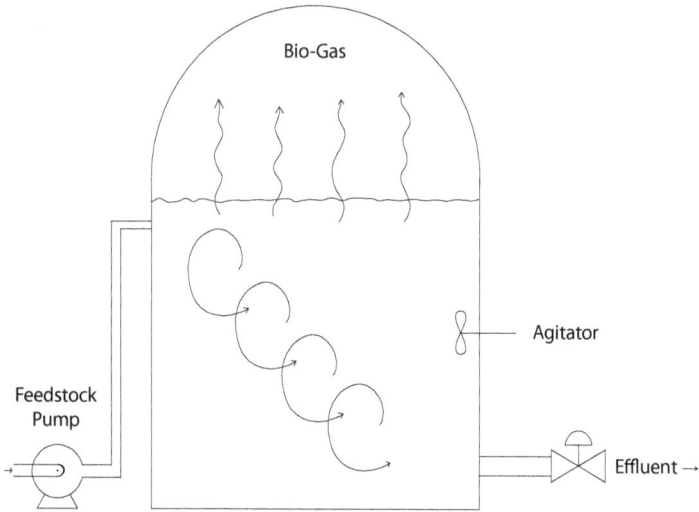

Although bio-digesting is a relatively simple process, there are several key parameters that must carefully be considered in the financials for an installation.

The first is the proximity to the available feedstock. Agricultural waste such as manure, crop scrap, and switch grass are all very good feedstocks. But if they are too far away from the facility, the trucking and transportation costs could become significant and outweigh the savings.

The second parameter involves the commodity pricing of the feedstock. Manure is essentially free for the farmer who owns the livestock, but may come with a price tag to someone who wants it to generate a profit. More importantly, is the outlook forecast. A feedstock that is relatively inexpensive today may not be 10 years from now. As additional bio-digesters are constructed, the demand for the feedstock could increase greatly over time. Your project may begin with the farmer paying you to take the feedstock, but evolve into a financial model where you are soon paying the farmer for the same feedstock.

The third parameter is diversity of the feedstock. With a bio-digester we often say, "In a plastic bag, out a plastic bag." If your feedstock is diverse, and contains inorganics such as plastic, gravel, metal, etc., these will need to be sorted and separated.

Finally, depending on your design (batch or continuous) and your feedstock, you will likely be left with "digestate" after the feedstock has been used and the methane has been captured. The digestate is a peat-like material that is often left in the bio-digester because it was too dense or fibrous to fully convert in the short, low temperature operating conditions. The good news is that the digestate is often rich in BTU value, and can be an ideal fuel for a waste fuel boiler. See the section ahead on waste fuel boilers.

Co-Generation

Co-Generation, or "CoGen", gets its name from producing two forms of energy from a single source of fuel. In the simplest of terms, a CoGen plant starts life very much like the jet engine on an airplane. But instead of hanging from the wing of an aircraft, the engine is stationary, mounted on the ground. The fuel (typically natural gas or syn-gas) is combusted in the turbine, which spins a generator to produce electricity. This alone is a very useful process, but the engine also generates a great deal of heat in its exhaust gas. On an airplane, the hot exhaust gas is simply liberated into the air as the plane flies through the sky. However, in Co-Generation, the hot exhaust gas is captured and re-used. The hot air can either be ducted to a process that requires large amounts of hot air, or it could be fed into a heat recovery boiler (HRB) to generate steam. It's the production of these two energy sources (electricity + heat) that gives "Co"-Generation, CoGen, its name. See also the following section on Tri-Generation (3 outputs).

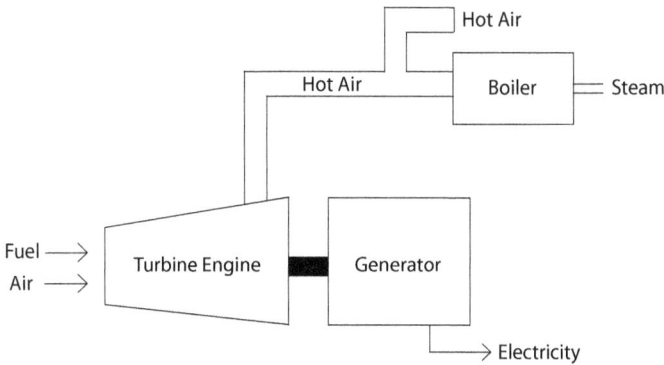

A well-designed CoGen facility can be installed today for around $1Million per MW (Megawatt). Although this is a very attractive installed capital cost, it is important to remember that the CoGen must be fed with Natural Gas, where some of the other technologies with a higher capital cost are "fuel free" once they are installed. Still, the $1 Million per MW cost of CoGen remains the benchmark to which most other technologies are often compared.

Concentrated Solar Power (CSP)

Concentrated solar power is the technology of using the heat from the sun to produce electricity through steam generation.

When most people speak of "solar power," they are usually referring to Photovoltaic solar (PV Solar), where solar panels are used to convert the sun's energy directly into electricity. See the "Solar Photovoltaic" section for more on this technology.

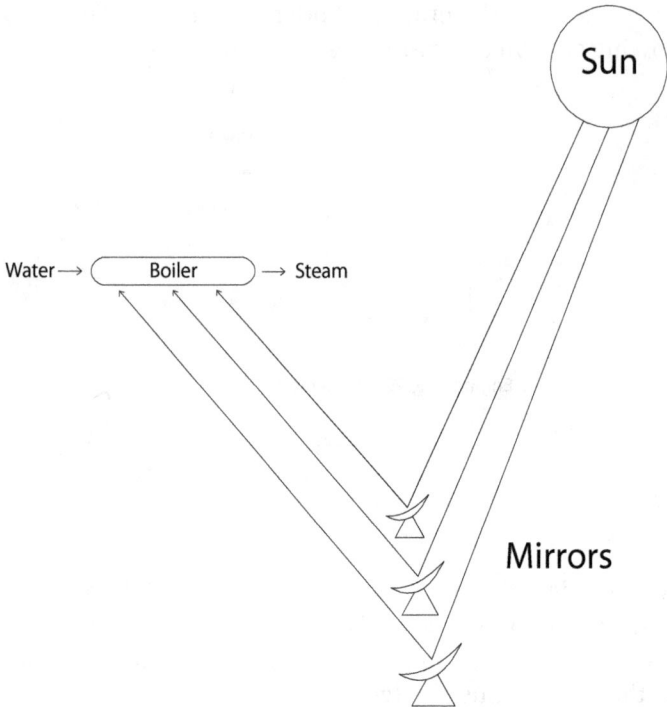

Sun

Water → (Boiler) → Steam

Mirrors

With CSP, there are no solar panels. Instead, a series of mirrors are used to reflect the sun's light and concentrate it on a focal point. That focal point becomes extremely hot and in turn boils water or generates steam. The steam can be used to spin a generator to produce electricity, or it can simply be used as a source for steam in a process plant.

As children, many of us took great satisfaction in using a magnifying glass to focus the sunlight onto a piece of paper.

After a short time of experimenting, we determined how far to hold the magnifying glass from the paper. Once we establish an intense orange dot, the paper would quickly begin to burn. This is very similar to the process in CSP.

CSP has cost benefits beyond PV Solar applications. The equipment to concentrate sunlight is typically far lower than that of solar panels. Also, recent developments in curved mirrors and GPS tracking of the sun have made this a very competitive technology. Furthermore, CSP is very versatile and allows for the production of hot water, saturated steam, superheated steam, electricity, or the combination of any of these. It is this flexibility that adds to the benefits of CSP. As with PV Solar, however, geographic location makes or breaks the technology based on sun intensity. And while the GPS tracking technology extends the useable sunlight by 2-3 hours per day, CSP still generates zero power in the dark.

CSP is very cost competitive, with some installations as attractive as $5 Million for a 7.5MW system. The output must, of course, be multiplied by the efficiency factor of the location being studied, but it remains a competitive technology that will grow more efficient in the years ahead.

CO_2 Sequestering

CO_2 sequestering is a technology that may be ideal for large manufacturing plants that are already in existence. An ideal example could be a CoGen facility that is under contract to generate electrical power, but must meet new legislation to reduce its CO_2 emissions. This is a double-jeopardy situation because the only way to comply with the new legislation may be to violate the power generation contract. In other words, their contract requires that they continue to use natural gas to generate electricity, but the new law requires that they reduce their emissions.

This is where CO_2 sequestration can help. It is an expensive option, but for some operating facilities, it might still be their best option.

CO_2 sequestration is just a fancy term for "removing and capturing the CO_2." What essentially happens is that the flue from the emission point is scrubbed of CO_2. The CO_2 is removed and captured, and no longer emitted into the air. And since the sequestration equipment is located downstream of the production process, it is not disruptive to the operation of the facility.

Although there are several technologies that do this today, the two most commonly used are the "solvent bath" and the "selective membrane." With the solvent bath technology, the flue gas passes through a bath of solvent, which the CO_2 favors. As a result of the relative solubility products, the CO_2 leaves the flue gas and remains entrained in the solvent. The solvent is then regenerated, causing the CO_2 to be released from it (usually with a temperature shift) and the CO_2 is captured and contained.

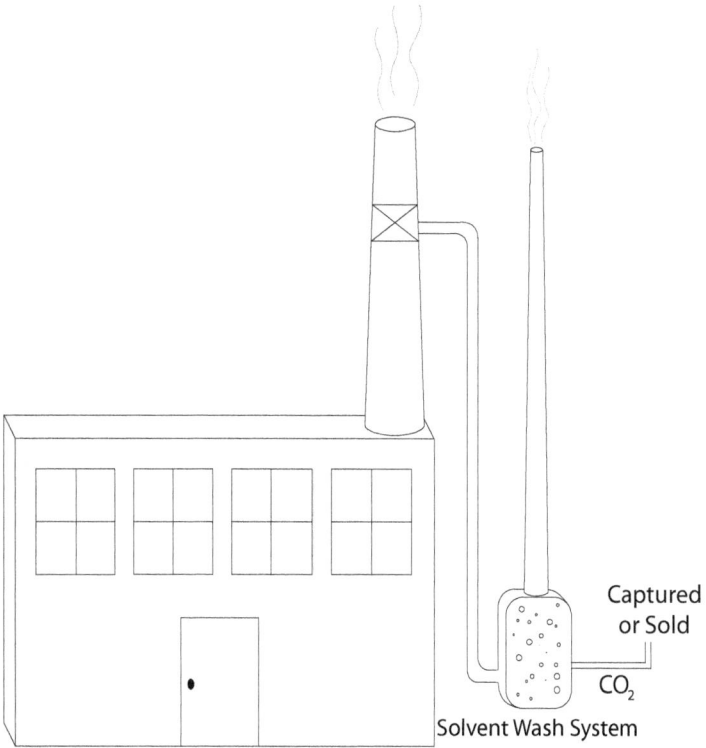

Captured
or Sold

CO_2

Solvent Wash System

With the selective membrane technology, a proprietary membrane is used in order to separate the gases due to their molecular sizes. A "delta P" is created across the membrane, and the various gases are separated. The CO_2 is captured and contained, while the remaining gases continue on.

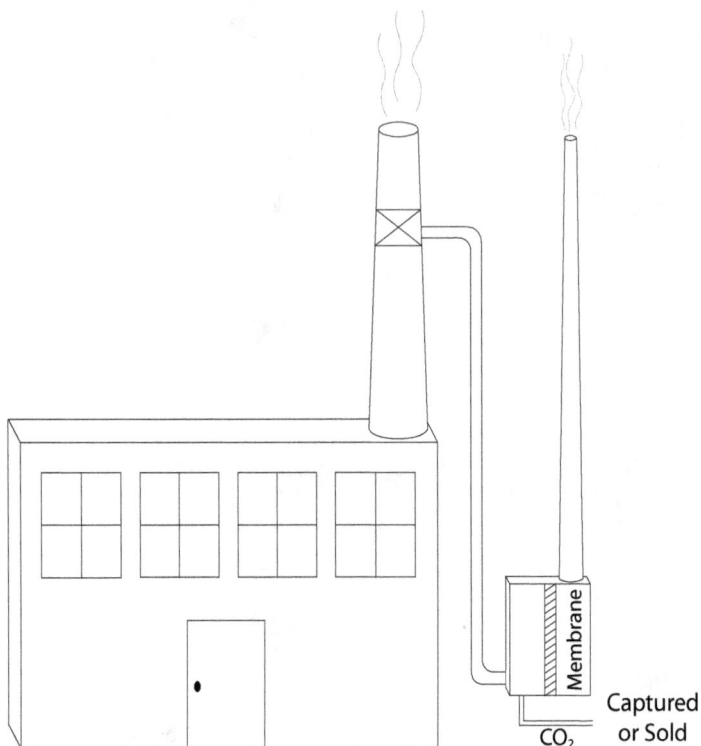

At this point you are probably wondering what happens to the CO_2 now that it is captured and contained. Believe it or not, many countries that use this technology simply pump the CO_2 deep into depleted oil cavities where it will never be released into the atmosphere. When the client's goal is to reduce man-made CO_2 in order to reduce climate change, this makes logical sense. However, if the client's goal is to honor their contracts, comply with the legislation, and maintain their profitability, there are many better uses for the CO_2.

CO_2 is a highly desired gas in many industries. Carbonated beverages (soft drinks, beer, sparkling wines) all purchase CO_2. Yes, to the true aficionado, the best beers and sparking wines should be naturally carbonated. But that is a small part of the total market. In addition, the recent growth in hydroponic greenhouses has increased the demand for CO_2, as these high-tech greenhouses pump CO_2 into the facilities to stimulate plant growth. Laboratories and other industries also use CO_2 in their processes, but food-grade CO_2 is the largest demand.

The financials for food-grade CO_2 seem to vary wildly, but that's because of the wide variety of sourcing involved. Focusing on industrial-quality, food-quality, or medical-quality drives much of the market pricing. But equally important are the compression and transportation costs.

Each situation must be carefully modeled for financial viability, but in many cases the CO_2 sales can generate enough revenues to justify the initial capital cost of the sequestration equipment.

Fuel Cells (Molten Carbonate)

Fuel cells are not exactly new, as they were initially demonstrated as far back as 1839. But today's modern fuel cells were advanced by NASA after 1959. Fuel cells are a remarkable technology that convert a supplied fuel directly into electricity. This is done in the cell at a molecular level, and there is no actual combustion of the fuel.

Fuels cells range in size from 1 kW to as high as 10 MW. There is an extraordinary line-up of fuel cells that are available today, but the most common are the alkaline, molten carbonate, phosphoric acid, exchange membrane, and solid oxide. For most manufacturing applications, the Molten Carbonate Fuel Cell (MCFC) appears to be a great fit.

Inside the fuel cell the reaction that occurs is shown by the following equations:

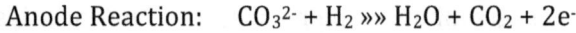

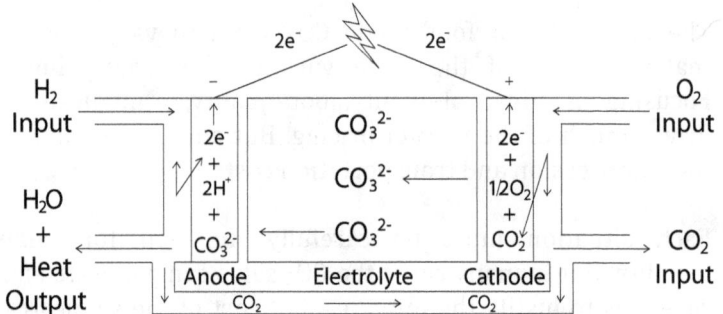

Anode Reaction: $CO_3^{2-} + H_2 \twoheadrightarrow H_2O + CO_2 + 2e^-$
Cathode Reaction: $CO_2 + \frac{1}{2}O_2 + 2e^- \twoheadrightarrow CO_3^{2-}$

$2e^-$ $\quad$ $2e^-$

H_2 Input $\qquad$ $-$ $\quad$ CO_3^{2-} $\quad$ $+$ $\qquad$ O_2 Input

$2e^-$ $\qquad$ $2e^-$

$+$ $\qquad$ $+$
$2H^+$ $\qquad CO_3^{2-} \leftarrow \qquad$ $1/2O_2$
H_2O $\qquad +$ $\qquad +$
$+$ $\qquad CO_3^{2-} \qquad CO_3^{2-} \leftarrow \qquad CO_2^{}$ $\qquad CO_2$ Input
Heat Output $\qquad$ Anode $\qquad$ Electrolyte $\qquad$ Cathode
$\qquad CO_2 \qquad \longrightarrow \qquad CO_2$

Through this reaction the fuel (typically H_2 and O_2) are reacted to release $2e^-$. This release of these 2 electrons is the generation of electricity from the fuel cell.

A common misconception is that fuel cells are interchangeable with batteries. Let's use a small fuel cell in a car to explain the differences:

A traditional electric car typically plugs in to a power source and charges the batteries. When you drive, the batteries are depleted, and you must eventually stop to recharge the batteries. Often, with today's technology, the batteries might propel you 150 miles or so before they require an 8-hour recharge. This makes long range driving very slow and difficult.

With a fuel cell, the vehicle is also an electric car, but instead of using batteries that are recharged by plugging them into a power source, the electric motor is fed with the electricity from the fuel cell. The fuel cell is fed from the hydrogen (H_2) from the fuel tank, so the driving range is only limited by the size of the fuel tank. And when refueling is required, it only takes a few short minutes and the vehicle is refueled and ready to continue its journey.

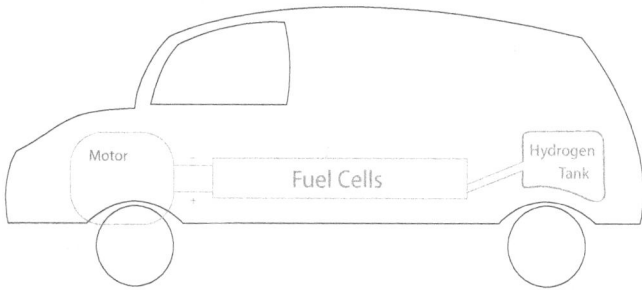

So in the simplest of terms, electric cars have batteries that are recharged by plugging them in. Fuel cell cars are the same as hydrogen cars, which are also electric cars, but with onboard fuel instead of batteries.

Molten Carbonate Fuel Cells cost roughly $4.5M per MW installed on the west coast. Although MCFCs are one of the most expensive technologies available to generate clean electricity, the rebates and incentives available in California can cover the majority of the cost of a Fuel Cell.

Fuel switching

Fuel switching can be a great way to reduce the energy costs in a facility. It is not often done, as it may compete with other goals that have been set. With fuel switching, a less expensive, but less efficient fuel may be "switched" in place of the more expensive, higher efficiency fuel. In this scenario, the fuel usage increases while the fuel costs decrease. In most of these cases the CO_2 generation often increases as well, since more fuel is being used.

When approaching this strategy, it is critical that the facility's leadership is crystal clear on their goals, and that these goals fit with their corporate goals and philosophies.

To illustrate how this works, let's look at a manufacturing plant located in the north central United States. The plant has several boilers on site, and they can utilize either coal or natural gas to fire them. On a BTU basis, the coal is cheaper than natural gas, even though it is less efficient.

The plant has a very strict policy to always operate within the confines of their environmental permits and to comply with all laws and regulations. Their current operating strategy directs them to utilize coal up to the limits of their permit, and then to utilize natural gas to make up the remainder of their boiler steam. This is the most cost effective way for them to operate within their permits.

The plant needs to remain competitive, so they must reduce their cost. But they cannot increase their coal usage and remain within their permitted levels.

The plant leadership brings in a fuel switching expert who models their production processes and mass and energy balances. Instead of disrupting the delicate manufacturing process within the plant, the team focuses on fuel switching. The boilers are left untouched. The manufacturing process is left untouched. However, in the utility department several changes are made. The scrubbers and bag houses are upgraded, and new pulverizers are installed. By installing the improved scrubbers and bag houses, the emission levels drop, offering an enlarged operating window for using coal. Furthermore, by installing an upgraded pulverizing system, the grade of coal could be expanded. Coarser, less expensive coal could now be purchased.

The savings from burning more coal and less natural gas, coupled with the reduced purchase price of the larger size coal produced a very attractive return on their investment. Their energy costs decreased, and they remained well within the permitted levels of emissions that had been established.

Yes, their actual fuel usage increased as their cost decreased (due to the BTU differences between the two fuels), and their carbon footprint increased (CO_2 was not regulated in their state). But their savings were significant, allowing the plant to stay competitive and protect the jobs of the 1500 employees that they employ.

Leading a manufacturing plant is often a very difficult job. In this real example, the plant manager balanced protecting 1500 jobs with the stigma of burning more coal. The parent company offset the CO_2 increase in their other plants, and the goodwill from the employees and their families spread through the community.

Although not the intended subject of this chapter, this example is also a case study in the balance of supporting the jobs in the community with improving the environment.

Geothermal Electricity

It is well known that the solid surface of the earth is essentially "floating" on a sea of molten lava. In very simple terms, if you drill deep enough, you will eventually hit hot rocks and lava. Costs can exceed $1 Million per mile, so this technology works best in regions of the world where the hot rock and lava are close to the surface.

Once the location has been determined, a series of pipes carry water from the surface down to the heat source, and then return the hot water or steam back up to the surface for use in a boiler or steam turbine to produce electricity. Although the cost of installation is quite high, once the Geothermal site is operational, there are essentially no fuel costs associated with running the plant. The subterranean heat source is endless, and the resulting electricity will have a zero carbon footprint.

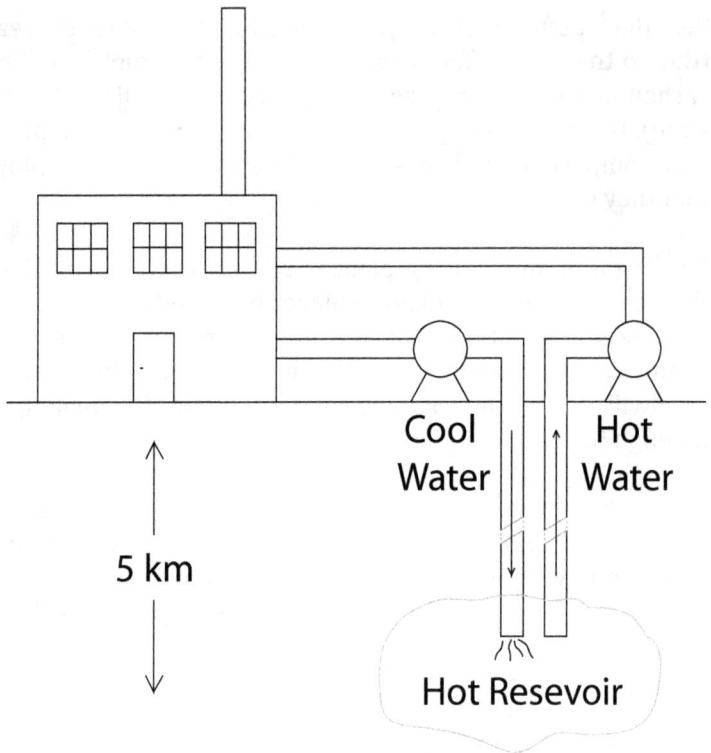

Cool Water

Hot Water

5 km

Hot Resevoir

Geothermal HVAC

Geothermal HVAC is using the stable "below ground" temperatures to reduce the Heating, Ventilation, and Air Conditioning (HVAC) costs. In some cases, a local river, lake, or waterway could be used as well.

The benefit of geothermal HVAC rests in the fact that temperatures 10-12 feet below the ground surface remain relatively stable. So in the summer time they are cooler than surface temperatures, and in the winter time they are warmer than the surface temperatures. Let's use an example to show how this works:

Summer Temp:	85 F
Winter Temp:	40 F
Geothermal Temp:	65 F

A Geothermal system on the client's property is essentially a system of tubes, pipes, and vessels that are buried below the ground. During the hot summer, the intake air for the air conditioning system is pulled through the buried system, so that it arrives at 65F. Since it is already cooler than the ambient air, the air conditioning system doesn't have to work as hard, so the cost decreases. In the winter season, the exact opposite is true. The intake air (through the same system) is now warmer than the ambient temperatures, so the heating system does not have to work as hard either.

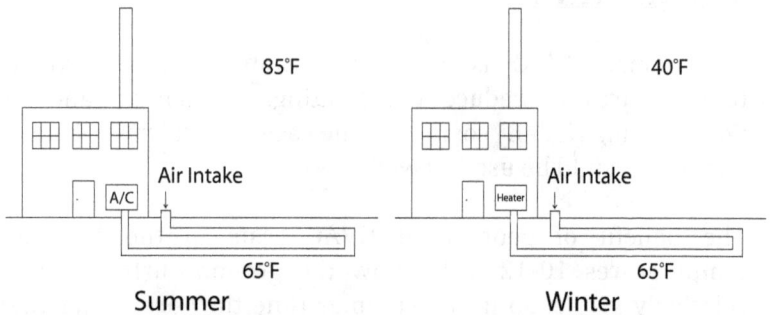

	85°F		40°F

Summer — Air Intake, A/C, 65°F

Winter — Air Intake, Heater, 65°F

Obviously, the depth of installation, the sizing, and the expected gains are very dependent on the geographic location of the facility, so precise benefits are beyond the scope of this section. It should also be noted that while day-one installations usually offer attractive returns, retro-fits become prohibitively expensive unless adjacent land is available for the installation.

Heat Recovery

Heat recovery is certainly a broad term, but it addresses one of the biggest opportunities in manufacturing plants. It is essentially free energy, because the fuel was already paid for and the CO_2 was already tracked during the first time that it was used.

The discussion of heat recovery could encompass an entire book of its own. And it would be a pleasure to write that book, because heat recovery is one of my two favorite energy topics (along with waste gasification). But sadly, many manufacturing operations do not understand heat recovery. As a result, they often pay for energy two or even three times to accomplish a single task.

Let's again use a real life example. A metal finishing plant operates in a large facility with a reduced number of operating lines. As recent as 10 years ago they operated 30 finishing lines, but with upgrades to the drives and automated robotics, they can now achieve the same production with only 12 lines. The 18 idled lines were left in place so that they could be started up in the event of a failure on one of the primary lines.

A critical part of the finishing process occurs when the metal is heat treated (for strength) in their tempering operation. Natural gas is used as the fuel to heat the heating blocks for the process. They use an "open" design so that the operators could view the process through the heating blocks. Because so much heat was given off at that station, the operators installed fans to blow the heat away from the station so that it could be dissipated into the large production room. In order to comply with the local labor laws, the building was climate controlled to 72F all year long.

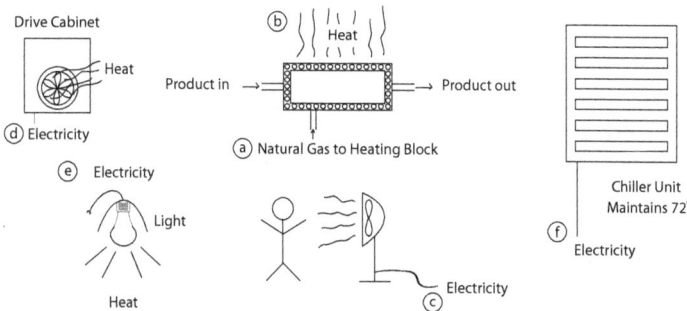

Although this process made complete sense to them at each stage as it evolved over time, the above paragraph should be setting off alarms and concerns for you. Let's go through what this:

a. Natural Gas is purchased to heat the finishing blocks
b. Waste heat is sent into the room
c. Electricity is purchased to run fans to dissipate the heat into a different part of the room

d. Electricity is purchased for all of the drive cabinets cooling fans that dissipate additional heat into the room
e. Electricity is purchased to power the ceiling lights above the idled 18 lines that shed light into unoccupied areas and dump additional heat into the room
f. Electricity is purchased to run chillers to cool the room to 72F

It is quite evident that the plant has purchased both electricity and natural gas to create energy that then needs to be removed by purchasing more energy.

Natural Gas is purchased to generate heat, and the left-over heat is dumped into the room. Next, electricity is purchased for the HVAC system to cool the room. Ironically, the cooler room has an impact on the heating block efficiency, which causes the need for additional natural gas.

This example is actually the norm more than the exception. A few simple changes will prevent their energy sources from competing with each other and reduce their energy usage, their energy costs, and their CO_2 generation:

- Install ducting over the heater blocks and divert the hot air directly up and out through the roof of the building
- Install a damper in the ducting so that the warm air is diverted into the room in the winter months
- Remove the floor fans
- Install ducting around the drive cabinets and divert the hot air into the primary ducting
- Turn off the lights above the idled lines; if the lights are fluorescent lights, be certain to throw the breakers to reduce electricity to the ballasts, which convert the electricity to heat even when the lights are turned off

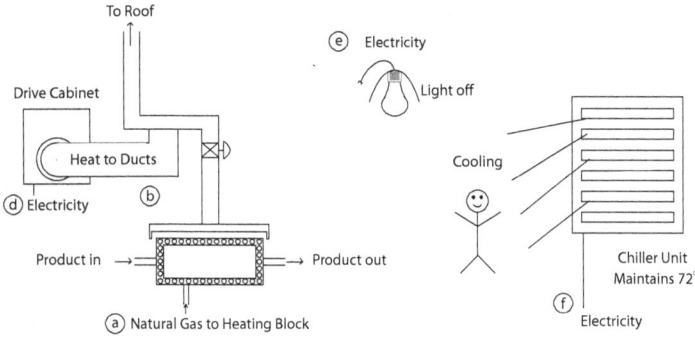

Drive Cabinet

To Roof

Heat to Ducts

ⓓ Electricity

ⓑ

Product in → → Product out

ⓐ Natural Gas to Heating Block

ⓔ Electricity

Light off

Cooling

☺

Chiller Unit
Maintains 72°

ⓕ Electricity

It's easy to dismiss this example because it sounds too crazy to exist, and too easy to resolve. But you would be surprised at how common this is.

Each transformation of energy (electricity to cooling, natural gas to heat, etc.) has an efficiency loss. No transformation is 100%. So not only are there wasted transformations, but there are efficiency losses that occur at each of these transformations as well.

High Efficiency Lighting

High efficiency lighting covers a broad array of available technologies. But the idea is simple:

a. Turn off the lights that are not needed (sensors, timers)
b. Reduce the wattage of the bulbs for constant lumens

This is a great place to start with any energy program, and it nearly always delivers positive results. Lighting has been a long ignored area of cost, and can therefore offer some relatively quick gains.

It is highly recommended that intermittent lighting be controlled by timers or motion sensors, as the lowest cost occurs when the light is actually turned off.

There have been some extraordinary advances over the past few years with high intensity fluorescents, induction lights, LEDS, and electronic ballasts.

Fluorescent tubes can quickly be upgraded to more efficient tubes with an immediate reduction in cost. Let's cover some brief nomenclature and then review a few of the easiest upgrades that are available today:

Fluorescent tubes are the most common indoor lights used in manufacturing and commercial buildings. The light usually has a designation like:

"F40T12"

This can be confusing, but it's really pretty straightforward:

F   = Fluorescent
40   = 40 watt
T   = Tubular
12   = The bulb size measured in 1/8" of diameter

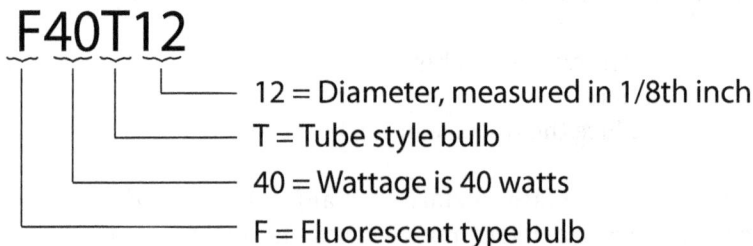

F40T12

- 12 = Diameter, measured in 1/8th inch
- T = Tube style bulb
- 40 = Wattage is 40 watts
- F = Fluorescent type bulb

That last indicator is the most confusing. Fluorescent bulbs are measured by their diameter, and that diameter is listed in 1/8's of an inch. So a bulb that is 1.5" in diameter would be 12/8", with the designation of T12. A 1" diameter bulb would be 8/8" and listed as a "T8" bulb. A 5/8" bulb would be listed as a T5 and so on. It's a bit of a strange way to measure the bulb size, but once you understand the nomenclature, it's pretty easy to follow.

Increasing the Lighting Efficiency helps in two ways:

a. It reduces the cost of your lighting
b. It reduces the cost of your A/C

The lighting savings is pretty easy to understand, as a 32 watt bulb should use less electricity than a 40 watt bulb. But the second savings must not be overlooked. From a pure physics standpoint, it is fairly accurate to state that all light emitted into an area is transformed into heat. With fluorescent lights this occurs at the bulbs as well as the ballasts. With incandescent lights it is primarily radiated at the bulb surface. Anyone who has touched a lit incandescent bulb can testify that the light is generating heat. And any young girl who had an Easy Bake Oven as a child knows that she can get enough heat from a light bulb to bake a cake.

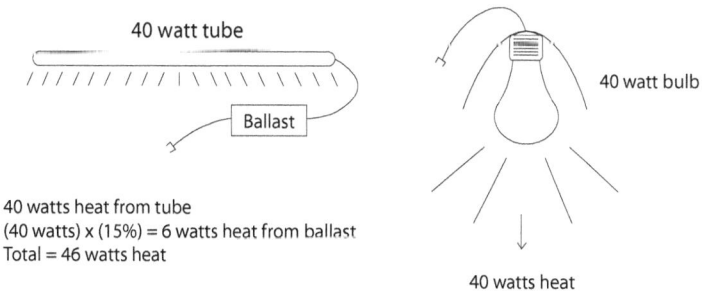

40 watt tube

Ballast

40 watts heat from tube
(40 watts) x (15%) = 6 watts heat from ballast
Total = 46 watts heat

40 watt bulb

40 watts heat

So if you have an office with 3 fixtures of 4 bulbs each, fitted with F40T12 bulbs, there is:

(3 fixtures) x (4 bulbs) x (40 watts) = 480 watts
There are 480 watts of heat entering the office. This is comparable to a small hair dryer blowing heat non-stop into the office.

By reducing the wattage of the lights, the heat that is generated from those lights is also reduced.

Simply moving from a T12 bulb to a T8 bulb can result in a 30% reduction in energy savings.

An additional area of discussion involves ballasts. In any fluorescent lighting system there are 3 major components: the bulbs, the ballasts, and the fixture. The ballast is the black rectangular box that restricts the current so that the bulbs don't destroy themselves. As the ballast performs this duty, it becomes very warm and dissipates that heat into the room.

Years ago, when a fluorescent light was turned on it would flicker for a few seconds and then finally illuminate fully. Over the recent years, quick-start ballasts became available which allow the bulbs to illuminate almost immediately. But there is a trade-off for this enhancement, and the trade-off is that the ballast is always energized. By keeping the ballast energized at all times, the lights can be brought on with the flick of a switch. This means that the ballast is always drawing current, and always dissipating heat into the room, even when the lights are turned off.

Ballasts can draw up to 15% of the bulb wattage whether the light is turned on or off. So a pair of 40 watt bulbs are really using:

2 x (40 watts for lights) + (.15) x (40 watts ballast) = 92 watts

This can be a point of confusion for many people during lighting improvements. If a good lighting plan is executed, the savings should be greater than the total wattage of the bulbs. If the A/C benefits are calculated, the savings can be shown to be even higher.

It's important to look at the seasonal temperatures, however, when calculating A/C loads and savings due to bulb wattages. Although it's true that during the summer months, the lighting improvements will reduce the electrical costs due to the A/C load, the opposite is true in the colder winter months. During the months where the facility is heated, the natural gas usage (or other fuel) will likely increase, as there will be less heating of the facility by the lights. Depending on the geographical location of the facility, as well as the relative fuel costs, this seasonal impact could be either a net increase or a net decrease in the facility's total HVAC cost.

The final discussion for fluorescent lights has to do with their life expectancy. This measurement is usually called a mortality curve, and it's very important to understand this for the type of lighting that is being installed.
Fluorescent bulbs have a relatively stable survival rate (>90% of bulbs still functioning) until they reach about 60% of their rated life. At that point, the survival rate drops sharply. Bulb mortality at 85+% of the rated life is roughly 25 times higher than bulbs at <70% of their rated life. Simply translated, this means that fluorescent bulbs should be replaced when they reach 80% of their rated life. Beyond that, the failures will occur very rapidly. Financially, it does not make sense to get that last 20% from the remaining bulbs.

If the new bulb's accompanying literature indicates a 20,000 hour rating, the bulbs should be replaced at 16,000 hours of operation.

Hydro-kinetic Power

Hydro-kinetic power is a wonderfully simple and clean form of power. It has been around for hundreds, if not thousands, of years. A simple example would be a paddlewheel on a shaft that extends into a stream or a river, where the moving water turns the wheel and shaft to roll a millstone to grind grain. A more complex example would be harnessing the water flow from Niagara Falls to spin generators, which in turn generate electricity. In fact, many Canadians refer to their electricity as "hydro."

Obviously, the power generation facility at Niagara Falls is well beyond the resources (or the needs) of a single manufacturing plant. But there are a myriad of opportunities between these two extremes.

Much simpler, but modern applications could include small water turbines submerged in rivers with flowing current.

Permitting with the local water authority is typically the biggest obstacle to installing such technology. But the water authority permitting typically applies only to stationary installation (permanently constructed in the river or waterway). A simpler option could be a mobile approach where the water turbines are mounted onto a barge or floating platform to avoid the permitting requirement.

Tidal technology is a form of hydro-kinetic power where the strong flow of the ocean water is converted into electrical or mechanical energy.

These are emerging and developing technologies. But their success will rely more on the water rights and permitting than they will on the ability of the technology to deliver clean, useable energy.

Hydro-kinetic technology is some of the oldest, most reliable, and cleanest energy that we have available to us.

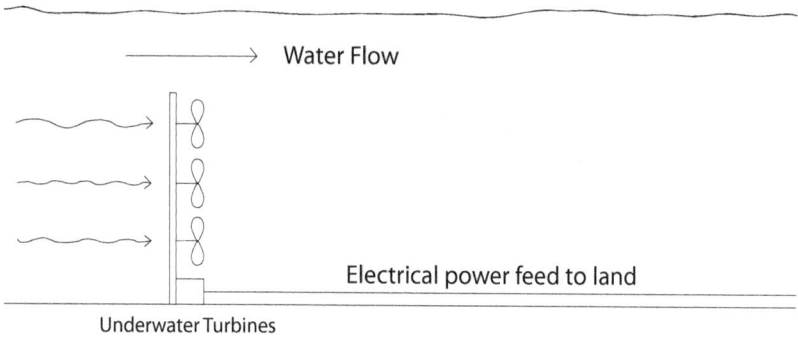

Underwater Turbines

LED Lighting

LED lighting has undergone remarkable advancements recently. Although LEDs have been around for a while, their lack of penetration (distance from light source to need) has kept them out of many potential applications. In areas with ceilings higher than 12-14 feet, the LEDs simply could not push the lumens down to the floor.

Today's LEDs are much more effective, and advanced cooling of the LED components has allowed greater intensity and extended life.

Another important improvement with LEDs has to do with the color of the light. Early LEDs offered a very blue light, which appeared unnatural to many people, but the newer LEDs have a color much closer to natural lighting.

LEDs are also offered in tube designs that can be placed into traditional fluorescent fixtures. The installation costs are remarkably low, as the fixture is already in place. The ballasts must be disconnected, of course, but it's still a pretty inexpensive conversion relative to replacing the entire fixtures.

Micro-Turbine Generators

Micro-turbine generators are a great technology, either by themselves, or when coupled with other technologies. A micro-turbine is a small (micro) turbine engine, typically in the 30-200 kW range. These turbines are often connected to a "micro-turbine generator" which produces electricity. In essence, they are small, compact versions of the units that are discussed in the Co-Generation and Tri-Generation technologies. Their distinguishing differences are often more than just their size. In addition to filling a segment of the market not met by the larger turbines (5MW+), there are micro-turbines in existence today that are remarkably simple, with only a single moving part. These simple designs are highly desirable, allowing them to be used in many commercial installations where size and cost are a limiting factor.

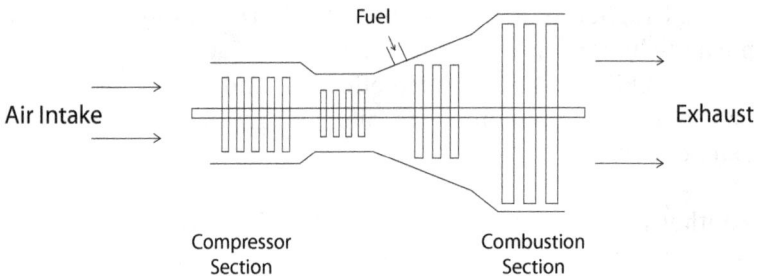

Fuel

Air Intake ⟶⟶   Exhaust

Compressor   Combustion
Section   Section

Even medium sized office facilities (>60,000 ft^2) in areas with high electricity costs can benefit from the spark spread of these compact units. Spark spread is the industry term used to differentiate the price of electricity and natural gas. A small 30 kW unit could generate 250,000 kWhs per year of electricity, while using the hot exhaust gases to offset boilers or hot water heaters.

Furthermore, these new micro-turbines are incredibly quiet, making about as much noise at 20 feet as a normal conversation would.

Organic Rankine Engines (ORCs)

Organic Rankine Cycle Engines, or simply Rankine Engines, have been around for a while, but have become increasingly more popular as electricity prices rise and their technologies advance.

An ORC typically uses a binary fluid in a closed loop to generate electricity. The fluid passes through a heat exchanger where it is exposed to a source of waste heat. Since the binary fluid (usually proprietary in composition) has a very low flashpoint, it quickly expands into a gas, increasing its volume. This expansion is used to create mechanical energy through any number of screw feeds, gears, or rotors. The rotating mechanical components are in turn connected to a generator, which produces the electricity. Once the expanded gas passes through the mechanical gear work, it cools back to a liquid state and the cycle continues.

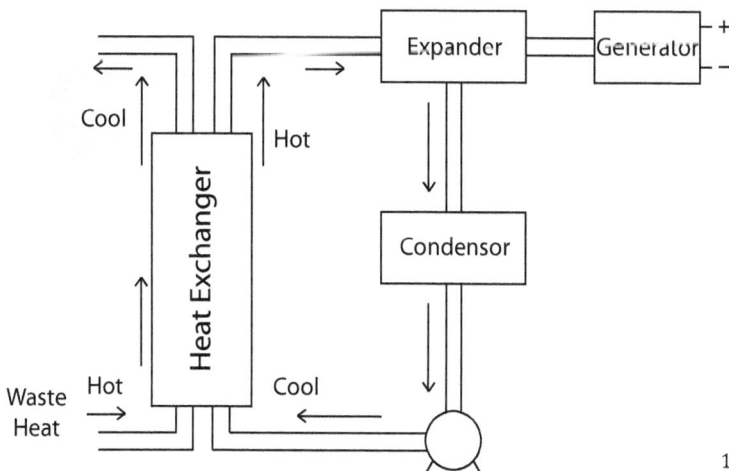

Today there are several very good manufacturers of ORCs on the market, and their sizes range from 30 kW up to over 1 MW.

The real benefit of these devices is that they produce clean, green electricity from waste heat. So they require no fuel, but simply run off the heat from a fuel that has already been purchased, spent, and released as heat. Furthermore, since they run off waste heat that might otherwise be discarded, they have no emissions from their production of electricity.

Pressure to Power (PTP)

Pressure to Power is not very common in the USA, but there are entire cities in Europe that run off PTP electricity that requires no fuel. PTP is the concept of converting stored energy, in the form of pressure, into mechanical energy, such as spinning an electric generator.

A simple example is an air wrench. An air compressor compresses ambient air and stores it in a tank. This is the stored (potential) energy. When you then use the air wrench to tighten the lug nuts on the wheels of your car, the stored (potential) energy is converted into mechanical energy to torque the lug nuts.

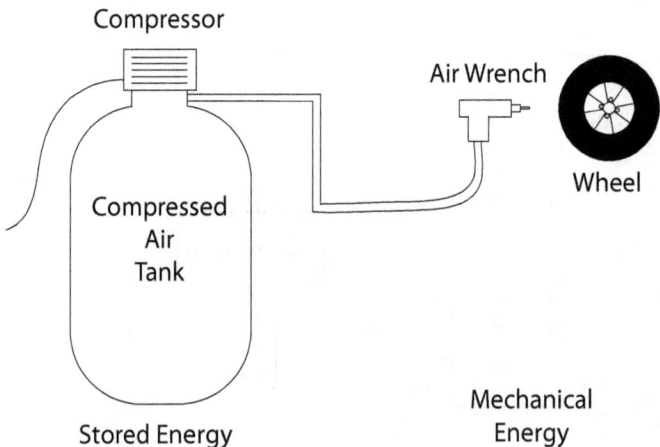

Compressor

Air Wrench

Wheel

Compressed
Air
Tank

Stored Energy

Mechanical
Energy

In the complete life cycle of this process, the stored energy is first created by a mechanical device, such as an air compressor. It is stored as compressed air and then converted back into mechanical energy. This process is very inefficient, as great heat is generated during the compression. Furthermore, there are two transformations that occur, and each of these transformations include an efficiency loss.

However, there are applications where the stored energy arrives without cost. The energy used for the compression may have been natural, or it may have been a necessary part of an upstream process.

As an example of this, let's think of a natural gas drilling well. Once the well is drilled deep enough to reach the natural gas, the gas travels up the pipe to the surface where it can be used as a fuel. But there's another opportunity there beyond the gas as a fuel. Let's say that the gas coming out of the ground is at 4000 psi. The "delta p" (difference in pressure between the high pressure gas and the atmospheric pressure) is enough to spin an engine or generator. If this is confusing, think about spraying a can of compressed air on a pinwheel. The can is similar to the natural gas pocket, and the nozzle of the can is like the pipe to the surface. The pinwheel is like a generator.

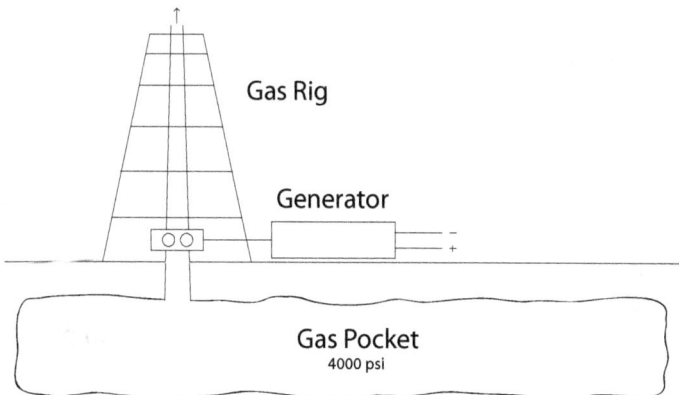

Gas Rig

Generator

Gas Pocket
4000 psi

As the gas at 4000 psi travels out of the ground, the pressure could be used to spin a generator to produce electricity. And keep in mind, that the resulting gas will retain its entire BTU value. The PTP energy comes from the pressure, not from the chemistry or combustion of the gas. It is free energy, benefiting from the compression that occurred naturally thousands of years ago.

Let's take a look at another similar example. Mike Toolman runs a manufacturing plant that is located in a rural area of Arkansas and uses a great deal of natural gas in order dry the product in his papermaking process. A main gas line runs to his property where it enters the reducing station, which lowers the pressures to the levels necessary in the plant. Let's take a look at this more closely. The 10" gas pipe that enters the reducing station is not remarkable in any way to the casual observer. But to the trained eye, it has money written all over it. That's because the pressure in that line might be as high as 800-900 psi. Mike understands that the utility company keeps the pressure very high so that they can reduce their costs. Mike's paper plant is located in a very remote area, far away from any cities. These gas pipelines could run literally hundreds of miles, and the cost of the pipe is very, very expensive. Mike thought about this for a while. He concluded that a smaller diameter pipeline would cost less for the utility company to install than a larger diameter pipeline. He was correct. But with a smaller diameter pipeline, they would need to increase the pressure to gain enough flow for Mike's plant. This wouldn't work very well with fluids like water or oil, but it works extremely well with natural gas.

So Mike now understands that he has 800-900 psi gas arriving at his property line, and this is significantly higher than the 55 psi gas that his manufacturing plant needs. In the reducing station on Mike's property the high pressure gas passes through a series of orifice plates, allowing the gas to expand and reduce pressure until it arrives at the desired 55 psi.

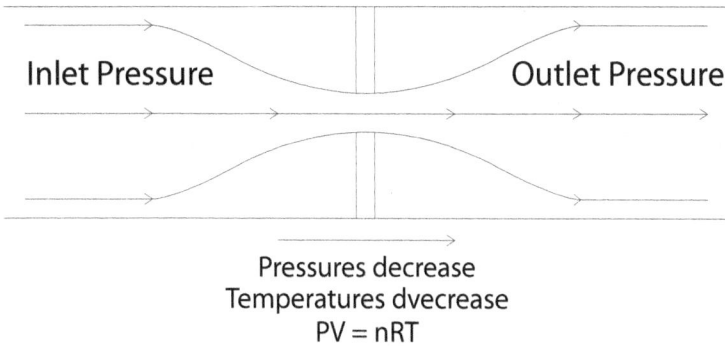

Inlet Pressure   Outlet Pressure

Pressures decrease
Temperatures dvecrease
$PV = nRT$

Very few people would ever go out to this utility station to look at it. But Mike is a very smart leader and is always looking for opportunity. Most people in his plant didn't even know that it's there. But as Mike took the time to go and look at it, he noticed two things immediately. First, it is very quiet, because there are no moving parts. Secondly, he noticed that there were several inches of ice on the pipes even though it was a hot, muggy, summer day at 90F. What's going on here?

It's called adiabatic cooling, and is technically a Joule-Thomson expansion. It is simply the phenomenon that when a gas expands, it gets cold. This has to be true because when a gas is compressed, it get's hot. The energy must be conserved. If you have ever sprayed a can of compressed air for a minute you will have noticed that the can gets cold. It happens every time. It's physics.

So what have we learned at this utility station? High pressure gas is reduced to lower pressure gas and there is a great deal of cooling that occurs. But how is it being harnessed? Sadly, it's usually not. It's simply being liberated into the environment (wasted).

What we want to do is to feed the high pressure gas into a mechanical engine, which rotates as the gas pushes through it. As that occurs, the gas pressure drops down to 55 psi, but the initial pressure is converted into mechanical energy, spinning a generator and making free electricity for the plant. And by the way, the cooling is also captured and used to air condition the offices in the plant. Free electricity and cooling from the delta p of the incoming natural gas!

PTP generators have not gained popularity in the USA, due in part because we have enjoyed an abundance of inexpensive electricity. However, this is changing for us. Areas of Europe have already implemented this technology. In fact, there are entire cities between Hamburg and Amsterdam that generate electricity from the natural gas that passes through the main lines near the city. To be clear, they are not using the natural gas to make electricity. They are using the flow and the pressure of the natural gas to make electricity.

There are several respectable manufacturers of this technology, and that provides a nice, competitive market. The early PTP engines were adapted from old steam engine designs, and function very reliably. Some have been in operation for over 40 years.

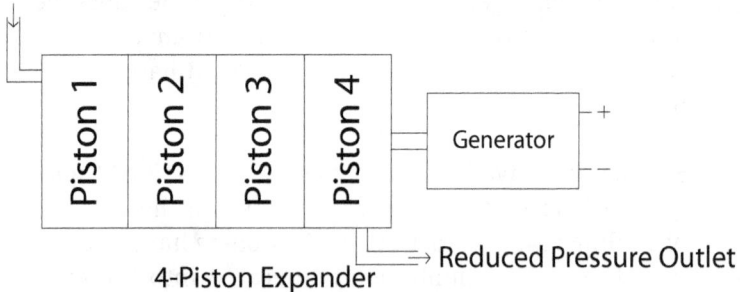

High Pressure Inlet

4-Piston Expander — Reduced Pressure Outlet

There is also a potential overlap with the ORC technology (see above), where the high pressure gas could be used in the ORC expander, generating electricity directly without the need for the binary fluid or the waste heat to flash the binary fluid.

There are obviously limited applications for this technology. But with large users of natural gas, where the utility station is on their property, this can be a marvelous technology to study and apply.

Solar Hot Water (SHW)

Solar Hot Water is the "no-brainer" of solar energy. It's simple, cheap, and if you live in the right geography, it's an easy relief to your bottom line. SHW relies on direct exposure from the sun and the fact that black absorbs heat. There are geographies (such as Mexico City) where you can literally see one on every residential property in the area. The units are typically placed on the roof and are simply plastic tanks the size of a hot water heater. Existing line pressure is used to replenish the water in the black tank, and the sun provides the heat to the water. When required within the home, the water feeds the source through the head pressure on the roof.

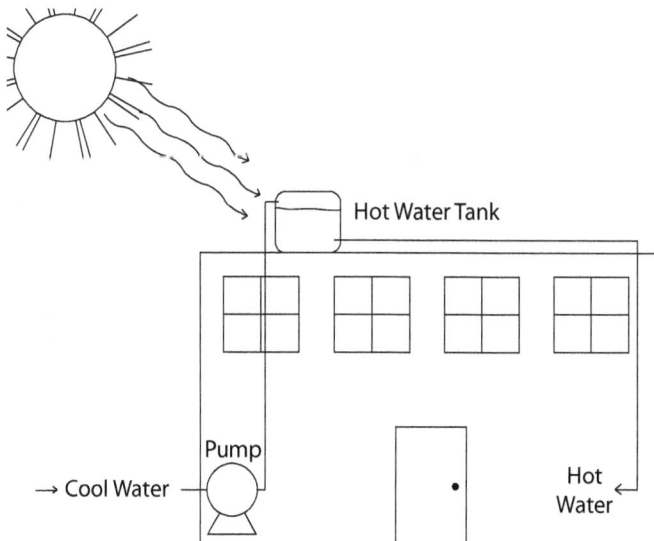

SHW will not provide steam or boiling water. But it will provide hot water if that is what is required. If a hotter source of water or even steam is desired, SHW is still a real cost savings because it provides pre-heating prior to a boiler or hot water heater.

It certainly doesn't work in all locations, but where it does, it's a great low cost solution with real bottom line savings.

Solar Photovoltaic (PV)

Photovoltaic Solar , or Solar PV is what most people are referring to when they simply say "Solar power." Photovoltaic derives its name from Photo (light) and voltaic (current) to describe the process of converting light into electricity.

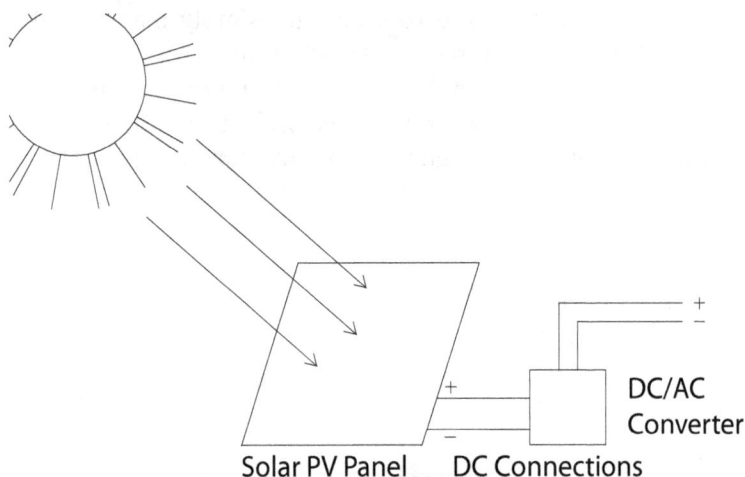

Solar PV Panel   DC Connections

Solar PV is well-proven technology with very low risk. The panels today are very reliable, most manufacturers offer very generous warranties, and the technology delivers what it promises. The drawback to Solar PV is typically the cost, which drives an extended payback period. It is not uncommon for

Solar PV to require 6-8 years to provide a return on investment at 6% capital. As a result, Solar PV is typically utilized in states where incentives and rebates are offered to offset the initial capital cost.

An additional opportunity is to utilize Solar PV through a Power Purchase Agreement (PPA). In this type of arrangement, a 3rd Party company purchases and installs the Solar PV panels and equipment on your property and then sells you the electricity. This is often an attractive option for companies that have high Internal Rate of Return (IRR) thresholds for savings projects. With a 6-8 year return on investment, these companies cannot take advantage of Solar PV. However, with a PPA, the client simply purchases the electricity at a rate comparable or lower to their current grid rate. The 3rd Party recovers their investment over a longer period of time and then makes their money in the later years of the PPA contract.

In a PPA scenario there are several options that allow the contract to be catered to the client. The "green" credits can be included in the PPA or they can be retained and monetized by the 3rd Party Company. Today's market could support a premium of $0.02/kWh for "green power." If the client doesn't have an interest in the green power, the PPA Company could sell green credits separately from the electricity sold to the client. They might sell the electricity for $0.11/kWh to the client, and then sell the "green" credits to another client for $0.02/kWh, increasing their total revenues to $0.13/kWh.

In addition, the contract can be structured in a way that undercuts the anticipated inflation of grid electricity. For example, the local utility provider may be forecasting a 6% per year increase in electrical rates. However, since the PPA provider will not "see" any inflation in their sun-powered panels, they may offer a 3% per year increase to the client. The PPA provider receives increasing revenues (at no cost) and the client protects themself from the rising energy costs. For many companies, this is an ideal scenario.

Swarm Technology – HVAC

Swarm technology is fairly new to the commercial market, and it has an incredibly high potential. The term "swarm" invokes the thought of bees all working together and flying in a formed fashion. This name is very appropriate, as this is essentially what it does.

Swarm technology is made up of hardware (retrofit) and software that coordinates the efforts of multiple Heating, Ventilation, and Air Conditioning (HVAC) units so that they work together. Since HVAC costs are one of the highest energy costs in many commercial applications, this coordination can provide significant savings.

Let's look at a large resort that is made up of lobbies, hallways, guest rooms, banquet rooms, conference rooms, and common areas. Most of these have their own thermostat controls so the guests can maximize their comfort. The guests in Banquet Room A, for example, set their thermostat for 70F, while the guests in Banquet Room B set their thermostat for 75F. Both Banquet rooms have their doors open to the hallway, where the thermostat is set at 72F. Since each thermostat is independent, it sends the proper signals to the respective HVAC systems to maintain the separate temperatures, each with equal priority, and each competing with the others.

HVAC 1

HVAC 2

HVAC 3

HVAC 4

Lights

Controller

Process Lead

Thermostat 1

Thermostat 2

Thermostat 3

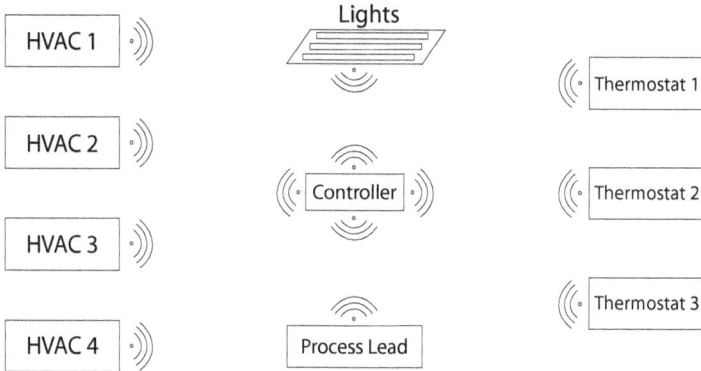

With swarm technology, the thermostats are all in communication with each other, and there is a hierarchy of set-points. They remain separate, but they talk with each other. Each individual thermostat is a part of the whole. The swarm technology could balance the cooler flows with the warmer flows to maintain the hallway temperature if that was a priority. However, if the priority was the VIP party in Banquet Room A, then the temperature setting for the hallway might be overridden to a lower temperature to support the desired 70F in the VIP party. Although each unit maintains its own inputted set-point, the lower priorities swarm together to best meet the needs of the higher priorities, as determined by the resort's leader.

Most swarm technology is designed to be retrofitted through wireless interfaces in order to minimize the initial capital cost. It is an amazing technology that can have an immediate impact on commercial HVAC costs.

Tri-Generation

Tri-Generation is a relatively new term that is used to describe an additional way to use the heat in a Co-Generation set-up. Technically, the Engine is still "Co-Generation" – creating the 2 sources of energy from one source of fuel. A Co-Generation (as described in detail in an earlier section) uses a single fuel, such as natural gas, to generate electricity and hot air. In a traditional Co-Gen plant, all of the waste heat is used as heat, either as hot air, or through a Heat recovery Boiler (HRB) to generate steam.

In a "Tri-Generation" design, the engine still makes the same amount of electricity and waste heat. However, only a portion of the hot air (waste heat) is used as a heat source. The other portion of the hot air is directed into a chiller to generate cooling. This is done through a specific type of chiller called an absorption chiller. With an absorption chiller, the hot air is directed into a heat exchanger where a fluid (typically ammonia based) is heated and flashed. The expansion of the ammonia generates the pressure to spin a compressor to create cooling.

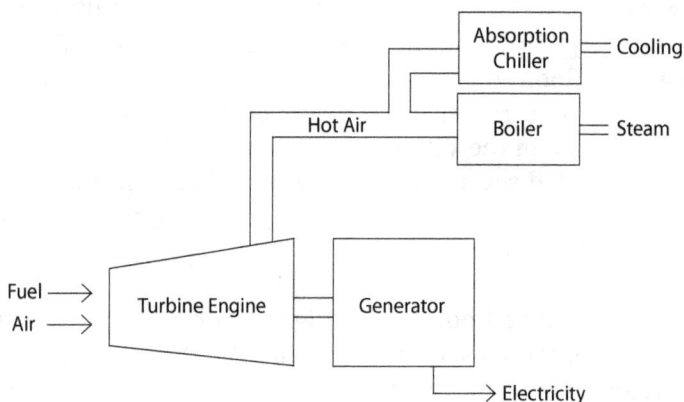

The set-up gets its name because the single installed project will generate electricity, heating, and cooling. Most importantly, the waste heat can be balanced or directed to make either additional cooling or additional heating. This can be a very powerful feature, as it can adjust easily to changes in seasonal climate temperatures.

The engine itself is still producing only heat and electricity, but the user gets a nice package of electricity, heating, and cooling.

This design can be an attractive set-up for commercial buildings, stores, warehouses, etc., if there is an attractive spark spread. Still, this technology has a much higher return on investment as a day-one installation than it does as a retrofit.

Waste Fuel Boilers (WFB)

Waste Fuel Boilers (WFB) are similar to gas-fired boilers. They use a fuel that is fed into the boiler, and the fuel mixes with oxygen (air) where it is combusted to generate steam. The steam from the boiler can then be used in its current state (for heating, process, etc.) or it could be used in a steam turbine to generate electricity.

The key difference with the Waste Fuel Boiler is that it is not using the traditional fuels such as natural gas, fuel oil, or coal. The fuel is a waste product, such as wood chips, bark, etc. The WFBs are considered much lower in equivalent emissions because their fuel is not a fossil fuel. The woodchips, for example, came from trees, which sequestered CO_2 during the life of the tree. The CO_2 that is emitted during the combustion of the wood chip returns the same CO_2 to the atmosphere that was sequestered as the tree grew. This natural process of absorbing CO_2 during the tree's growth and later releasing CO_2 as the tree decays is often called a CO_2 cycle. In this particular example, the CO_2 cycle is well short of the 100-year threshold, so it is considered a closed loop.

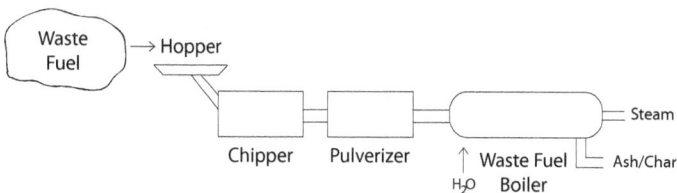

Waste Fuel → Hopper

Chipper   Pulverizer   Waste Fuel Boiler   Steam
H_2O Ash/Char

Fossil fuels are technically closed loop as well, since the petroleum had once been plant life that sequestered CO_2 while it grew and flourished. As the fossil fuel is burned, it releases the same CO_2 that was sequestered previously during the plant's life. The difference, of course, is time. The fossil fuels have a CO_2 cycle of perhaps 10,000 years or more, and today's politics restrict the CO_2 cycle to a 100-year limit to be considered green. As a result, fresh plant waste is considered carbon neutral, but ancient plant waste is not considered carbon neutral.

A WFB can be an efficient and green solution if there is an adequate supply of bio-mass. However, WFBs suffer some of the same limitations for fuel that were discussed earlier for Bio-Digesters.

A feedstock that is relatively inexpensive today may not be 10 years from now. As additional WFBs are constructed, the demand for the feedstock could likely increase greatly over time. Your project may begin with the feed source paying you to take the feedstock, but evolve into a financial model where you are soon paying the source for the same feedstock. Even today, most WFBs are operated with bio-mass fuel that is purchased from a local source.

Waste Gasification

Waste Gasification is my other favorite technology (along with Heat Recovery). It is a growing field due to advances in vaporization technology, metallurgy, and process control. But the biggest reason for the advancement in waste gasification is due to the demand. Put simply, waste gasification solves multiple problems with a single technology.

Over the past few years we have seen emission standards on fossil fuels tighten. We have also seen the local landfills in our communities become filled and capped. CO_2 emissions are becoming the fodder of Cap and Trade, and are already being regulated. And finally, our growing population and lifestyle requires a growing supply of electrical power.

This is where waste gasification really shines. With one application, a waste gasification facility:

a. Reduces solid waste to landfill by using Municipal Solid Waste (MSW) as a feedstock
b. Creates clean electricity for the community
c. Reduces the dependency on fossil fuels
d. Reduces CO_2e by converting landfill waste into electricity before it decays and releases methane into the atmosphere

This almost sounds too good to be true. Municipal Solid Waste (MSW) presents a number of challenges in order to be converted into usable electricity. And these challenges are not trivial. But they can and have been conquered. The current foot race is to be able to build a facility to do this with an attractive return on investment.

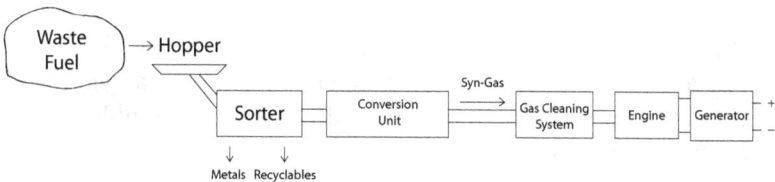

There are a number of technologies available to do this today, and each have their strengths and weaknesses. But the common thread through each of them is to utilize the technology in private business in order to generate revenues that are larger than the expenses. Thankfully, several technologies are on their victory lap in this regard.

The waste gasification sector has several emerging technologies. In the following pages, we will review some of the front runners.

Plasma Torch

Plasma Torch technology has by far the coolest name, and it utilizes one of the most advanced technologies in the line-up. Plasma is considered a fourth form of matter. When we heat a solid, it becomes a liquid. When we heat a liquid, it becomes a gas. But when we continue to heat a gas, we create plasma.

With the plasma torch technology, the feedstock is subjected to a plasma torch, which vaporizes the solid directly into a gas. It is critical that this occurs in an absence of oxygen so that no combustion of the feedstock occurs. This resulting gas is considered a synthetic gas, or syn-gas, and can then be used as a green fuel. More often than not, it is used as a fuel for an engine and generator to produce electricity.

Liquid Metal Bath

With liquid metal bath, the feedstock is cleverly injected into a vat of molten metal. Since the feedstock enters the bath below the surface of the bath, it is also converted in the absence of oxygen. The feedstock is quickly converted into a syn-gas by the hot liquid metal, and the resulting syn-gas bubbles to the surface and is captured for fuel.

Steam Reformation

With the steam reformation technology, the feedstock is introduced into a heated kiln, where the material is heated in the absence of oxygen by the walls of the kiln. The feedstock, as with the other technologies discussed, converts from a solid material into a useable syn-gas.

Each of the available technologies today have their particular strengths and weaknesses. Time will determine which of these technologies (or others) will command the future market. For now, each offers something special and unique, and is driving quickly to make their technology a viable and affordable one for their eager clients.

The financial model for waste gasification is fairly complex. The key revenues/incomes include:

1. Tipping fees (payment to receive the waste)
2. Sale of the syn-gas
3. Sale of the offset credits
4. Sale of the by-products
5. Sale of the electricity

The key variables in making the financials work for a waste gasification plant are:

1. Capital cost
2. Operating cost
3. Parasitic load of the plant
4. Local grid price for electricity
5. Local landfill cost for waste
6. Available government grants
7. Environmental permitting in the local area

It may be surprising to learn that it is not the advancement of the technology that is holding these projects back. Rather, it is the ability to permit these facilities and classify them in a way that helps the local communities while allowing them to operate successfully.

Alternative Fuels to Win

Alternative and Advanced Fuels provide powerful options and choices for any business that wants to reduce their CO_2e emissions. In some cases there may be a cost savings, but in most cases there is a premium to use these fuels.

However, in an AB32 world, the premium for the innovative fuels may be cheaper than the cost of purchasing allowances or credits. This will be discussed in much further depth in "Financing to Win," where the costs and savings of each of these options come together.

Alternative and Advanced Fuels will be defined as any fuel other than grid electricity, natural gas, fuel oil, or coal.

The benefits of Alternative and Advanced Fuels are that they carry a much lower carbon footprint than traditional fuels. But there are many ways to define their carbon footprint, so some pre-work may be required to insure that they deliver the desired results.

Let's begin with some background on carbon footprints and why they may be open to interpretation. If a tree is harvested and the resulting wood chips are used as a bio fuel, does it have a lower carbon footprint than a similar tree that died ten thousand years ago and was converted into petroleum? Both sequestered (absorbed) CO_2 for their entire life cycle. When they are burned for fuel, the chemistry says that they will release CO_2 back into the air.

They are only different because we have established regulations and definitions that say that they are different. It is commonly accepted that a "life cycle" within 100 years is considered to be sustainable, replenishable, and with a "very low carbon foot print." Fuels that fall into this category include such things as wood chips, bio-mass, bio-digested methane, etc. It should be noted that the sun's energy (via solar technologies) falls into the low-carbon footprint category, even though the sun's life cycle is well beyond 100 years.

The technologies that are associated with utilizing the "low-carbon footprint fuels" include boilers, waste fuel boilers, anaerobic bio-digesters, steam reformers, waste gasification, etc.

In many cases, advanced fuels (synthesized fuels) can be mixed with existing fuels to reduce the carbon footprint of the operation. A good example of this is pelletized bio-mass. Pelletized bio-mass is made by the supplier though a proprietary process of mixing the correct organic materials together to create a pelletized fuel with the desired BTU value. These pellets can then be blended into a coal-fired boiler to reduce the required amount of coal to fire the boiler. In most cases the blended fuel will be a fraction of the total fuel, possibly 10-15%, but it could be enough to reduce the overall carbon footprint by 10-20%.

Although there would be a fuel cost increase over using only coal, the equipment changes to blend the new fuel would be minimal, and the upcharge might be more attractive than other options available to reduce CO_2e.

Due to the SAR/AR4 factoring involved with the CO_2e calculations, there are actually fuels today that have a "negative" carbon footprint. Bio-char is a great example of this. Municipal Solid Waste (MSW), when used in the proper reformation technology can have a "negative" carbon footprint as well.

The Alternative and Advanced Fuels available today are advancing rapidly, making it difficult to explore completely within the scope of this book. However, these fuels should be a serious consideration for any business that needs to reduce their carbon footprint.

Current Fuels	Possible Replacements
Natural Gas	Bio-gas, Syn-gas
Grid Electricity	Wood chips, pelletized fuels
Coal	Wood chips, pelletized fuels
Fuel Oil	Wood chips, pelletized fuels

Resources to Win

In order to win at AB32, you will need to deliver strong, measurable results, and you will need to do it fairly quickly. The best way to accomplish this is through 3 sets of resources:

1. Internal resources to staff and execute the program
2. External resources to coach and train and then leave
3. External technology firms that install and then leave

It is often necessary to bring in external resources or consultants in order to start a new Sustainability Program. But they should be thought of as Coaches and Trainers who must eventually leave. They must not stay.

Let's review each of these 3 groups in more detail:

Internal resources to staff and Execute the Program

The ongoing leadership and execution of any Sustainability or Energy Conservation Program must come from within a company. It simply cannot be contracted out, or led from the outside.

External resources to Coach and Train and then leave

It is often a good idea to bring in skilled, experienced resources to help create and kick-off a new program. This can dramatically reduce the start-up time of the new program by tapping into deeper experience and expertise. The external resources can help the company avoid the pitfalls and mistakes of other "first-time" programs, as well as helping to reapply existing templates, tools, and documents so that they don't have to be re-invented with each new launch.

But these external resources must be focused on coaching and training, and then they must leave. They absolutely must leave. In today's business environment, we operate with a struggling economy, productivity demands, increasing taxes, and uncertain health-care regulations. It is tempting to bring in high-powered consultants and then retain them to execute the program. In theory this sounds good. But in practice, it will rarely work.

The resources must be focused on growing the skills internally to the company, reducing the need for the consultants themselves. Although this may sound counter-productive for those external consultants, it is the only strategy that is in the best interest of the company. The role of the consultant *must be* to build the internal skills within the client's company to the point that the consultant is no longer needed. It must be short-lived. Many consultants won't agree to this. But the best consultants won't agree to anything else.

External technology firms that install and leave

The third group is the external resources that are brought in to execute specific tasks. They are not expected to lead, coach, or drive the culture change. They are brought in to execute a specific project (*not* program) and then leave.

This group is easier to have leave because of the nature of their work. There is a clearly defined start and end to the project, and once the project is installed, the resources can leave. Examples of these resources include solar installations, carbon-credit brokering, air compressor installation, high efficiency lighting installation, etc.

Financing to Win

Winners play by the rules. But when necessary, they also update or change the rules to match the business situation.

Most operating businesses have a set of defined accounting practices that they require for all company personnel to use. They usually include standards for IRR thresholds, % capital for IRR/ROR calculations, and depreciation schedules. These are all very good things. However, in an AB32 world, there are 2 finance standards that must be updated or changed. This must always be done by key leaders in the organization and must be done prior to the first CO_2e reduction project. The 2 standards that must be modified are:

1. Definition of Savings versus Cost Avoidance
2. Inclusion of Revenue Streams into the Cost Model

Bear in mind that different businesses use different terminology, so it is important to use these concepts within the terminology that you have.

<u>Definition of Savings versus Cost Avoidance</u>

Many companies set aside a special fund for "Savings Projects." These are projects that have an initial capital cost (CapEx) with a resulting decrease in operating cost (OpEx). An example would be replacing all of the incandescent light bulbs with compact fluorescent bulbs. There is an upfront cost to purchase all of the bulbs, but from that point forward there is a decrease (savings) in the electricity bill.

Unfortunately, many companies do not recognize the concept of "Cost Avoidance." With a cost avoidance, there is no actual savings that occurs. The cost will not go down. Instead, the cost avoidance prevents the cost from going up. An example is a leaky pipe. There is no savings involved in paying $200 for a plumber to fix a leaky pipe. The cost is viewed only as an expense, without a corresponding return. However, if you *knew for a fact* that the leaky pipe would break next year and cause $3000 in water damage to the equipment nearby, it would be a true savings because it would be a true cost avoidance.

With AB32, businesses *know for a fact* what they must do. The covered entities have registered in CITSS. They know their required reduction of CO_2e under the law. They also know the cost of purchasing allowances or offsets if they do not reduce their CO_2e. From that point forward, they should be able to justify the cost of CapEx or OpEx based on the cost avoidance of purchasing allowances or credits.

This is a key shift for winning with AB32. But it is a difficult shift for most finance managers. And in a corporate world, the accounting practices must be consistent across all of the plants at all of the locations. This is a very important change to make. But do not underestimate the time and resources that might be required to make this change.

Inclusion of Revenue Streams into the Cost Model

Nearly all small businesses understand the concept of profit and loss. However, as businesses grow into corporations, the model that they use becomes increasingly complicated. With multiple locations, geographies, and currencies, the impacts of income, expense, depreciation, amortization, taxes, offsets, advertising, marketing, insurance, etc., convert a simple Profit/Loss model into a sophisticated system.

To simplify this, many companies have moved to a simple Cost Model. This allows the resources to focus on the things that they control. In manufacturing plants, the plant managers typically have 3 cost areas in their control:

1. People cost
2. Energy Cost
3. Material Cost

Their people costs are determined by how many people they have and how much they are paid. The material costs in the plants are usually driven by scrap rates, inventory, and remnants. The sourcing of the materials is typically done centrally, outside of the plant environment. Energy costs are driven by equipment utilization, downtime, and scrap/re-work rates.

Each of these 3 costs combine to create the plant's Manufacturing Operating Expense (MOE). This is very important. From this point forward the plant manager's reward system is typically geared towards the plant's MOE. There are, of course, other metrics such as Quality and Safety, but for this discussion the focus is on "Financing to Win."

So you might ask yourself, "Where are the revenues?" Well, in many corporations, the revenues are not driven by the local plant manager. Rather, they are driven by a separate sales force that operates centrally and allocates the volume to the plants. And, more often than not, the plants with the lowest MOE get most of the incremental production volume. It makes perfect sense. It is simple and logical.

But in an AB32 world, this Cost Model will prevent good projects and technologies from being executed.

Let's look at a small waste gasification plant for example:

Capital Cost:	$25 million
Operating Cost:	$4 million
Cost of electricity:	$0.12 per kWh

In a conventional Cost Model analysis, the IRR/ROR will be significantly negative. There is an upfront cost of $25 million. And from that point forward there will be a loss to the business every year, because they will be producing electricity from syn-gas at $0.12/kWh when they could purchase it directly from the grid for $0.08/kWh.

The project is assessed and discussed by the plant manager and the plant finance manager, and they quickly agree that the technology is not worth pursuing. It is just too expensive.

But their analysis is wrong. They followed their accounting standards and accounted for the CapEx ($25 million), OpEx ($4 million), and the Savings (negative $0.04/kWh). But they used the wrong Model. They used a Cost Model.

They should have used a Profit/Loss Model (P/L Model).

With the P/L Model they would have taken several other important factors into account:

1. Feedstock Tipping Fee ($1.7 million)
   The Tipping Fee is what the Waste Management Company would pay them to accept the MSW. Today that tipping fee is paid to the landfill site; in the future that $70/tonne would be paid to them

2. Sale of Bi-product ($0.6 million)
   The waste gasification technology generates significant amounts of high quality ammonia, which is sold as

fertilizer to the local markets

3. CO_2e Credits ($1.5 million)
The gasification plant generates twice the CO_2e credits than CITSS specifies for them. These can be monetized (sold) to other companies as offsets

4. Cost Avoidance of Purchased Credits ($1.5 million)
Without the gasification offsets, the base plan would be to purchase allowances or offset credits

The CapEx and OpEx are still the same. However, there are now revenue streams and cost avoidances totaling $5.3 million. They now make the assessment over a 5-year period:

Purchase allowances	$7.5 million cost
Waste Gasification Plant	$26.5 million income

Now the plant manager and the plant finance manager think that this is a great idea. And they would be right.

A final source of financing that should be taken into the P/L Model includes rebates, grants, and incentives. While these require some work to acquire, many states, especially California, are rich with funds to support sustainability and green technologies.

Conclusion

Winning with AB32 is a choice. It is a choice to go beyond the CO_2e reductions that are deployed by CITSS and to monetize the offset credits.

This is not a theoretical study of what might be possible someday. Companies are already doing this.

On August 5, 2013 the American Carbon Registry issued the first California Registry Offset Credits. There were 300,000 credits developed by Environmental Credit Corp under CARB's ozone depletion substances (ODS) compliance protocol. This first pool of offset credits will sell for approximately $4,500,000.

The Winners are already creating revenue streams as you read this book. The Losers are becoming slaves by purchasing their indulgences.

The rules that allow for Winners and Losers occur through the credits that can be traded either at the CARB auctions as allowances or between private parties as offset credits. In order to win in this game, a business should never buy CO_2 credits. But it should always work to sell them.

The Winners will be the businesses that implement a sustainability program and reduce their CO_2 emissions *beyond* what is regulated.

This is not about hugging trees. It's about increasing your profits and growing your business.

The key to doing this is implementing a sustainability program instead of just executing sustainability projects. Smart company leaders already know this. The others will figure it out too late. But the real winners will be the ones with enough vision to set goals well beyond the AB32 requirements, and then monetize the reductions. They will sell the reductions as offset credits to other businesses in California to create a new revenue stream for themselves. Once they understand how to use this new revenue stream as part of the financials in their own sustainability program, the revenues will be used to fund additional projects, creating even more revenue streams. These businesses will quickly learn that by executing a successful program once, they can create recurring CO_2 offsets that can be monetized year after year.

The Losers will stand in line to buy these offsets, and once the game gets going, it will be too late for them to do much of anything else. The Winners will be all too happy to sell them their salvation.

Legislation and Regulations come and go, but "Saving Money never goes out of Style".

The businesses that choose this strategy are the real Winners. And you can take that to the bank.

Glossary

AB 32   Assembly Bill 32 – "Global Warming Solutions Act"

ABCPTW   Auction Bidders Conference and Participant Training Webinar

AAR   Alternate Account Representative

ACC   Advanced Clean Cars

ARB   Air Resource Board

Binary Fluid   A fluid made up of several chemicals, which creates a characteristic very different from the separate components

Btu   British thermal unit (The energy required to raise the temperature of one gallon of water by one degree F)

CARB   California Air Resource Board

CITSS   Compliance Instrument Tracking System Service

CO_2 Carbon Dioxide

CO_2e Carbon Dioxide Equivalents; CO_2e allow for the comparison of all GHG (Green house gases) by using their molecular formulas to convert them into a common metric

COPs   Compliance Offset Protocols; these are developed by CARB to regulate the trading of offsets

Covered Entity	A company that is required to register in CITSS
ECI	Energy Consumption Index (Defined as the current energy per standard unit of production divided by the base energy per standard unit of production
EJAC	Environmental Justice Advisory Committee; This Committee was created to advise CARB in the Cap & Trade matters of AB32
ETAAC	Economic and Technology Advancement Advisory Committee
Flash point	The temperature at which a volatile material moves from liquid to gas
GHG	Green House Gases
Holding Limits	The maximum number of allowances that a company can hold
HVAC	Heating, Ventilation, and Air Conditioning
Instrument Vintage	The first year that an allowance is valid
Interplant	A manufacturing term used to describe how components are transferred between multiple plants to form a single product
kW	Abbreviation for kilowatts (1000 watts)
kWh	Abbreviation for kilowatt-hours (1000 watts for one hour)
Market Monitor	An entity charged with watching and summarizing the activities of the Auctions

MBDAA	"Market-Based Declining Annual Aggregate"; The Cap & Trade Program became the vehicle that CARB adopted
mcf	Abbreviation for 1000 cubic feet ("m" refers to roman numeral "m" and is often mistaken to mean "million)
mmbtu	Abbreviation for one million btus (each "m" refers to 1000, so 1000 times 1000 equals one million)
MMTCO$_2$e	Million Metric Tonnes of CO_2 equivalents
MSW	Municipal Solid Waste (Curb-side trash)
MW	Abbreviation for Megawatt (1 million watts)
Pavely 1	The revision to the 2020 GHG emission levels due to the impact of "advanced clean cars"
PAR	Primary Account Representative
Permaculture	The science of using a natural approach to harvesting resources from the land
PTP	Pressure to Power
Purchase Limits	The limits set by CARB to limit purchases by auction participants
Resource Shuffling	The movement of CA CO_2 outside of the state
RPS	Renewable Portfolio Standards
Scoping Plan	The Plan that CARB was directed to develop to explain how to achieve AB32's

goals through regulations, market mechanisms, etc.

SKU	Stock Keeping Unit
Syn-gas	Abbreviation for synthetic gas
Therms	A measurement for natural gas, which is equal to 100,000 btus Also equal to burning 100 cubic feet of natural gas
YAG	An odd abbreviation for a Year Ago